I love listening to Steve Timmis teach[...] Steve writes. He has become somewhat [...] Dei Church. In *I Wish Jesus Hadn't Said That*, this humble, witty, honest, and wise sage explores some of the hard sayings of Jesus and makes them clear and compelling. If you are looking for a basic discipleship book, some fresh sermon material for a study in the Gospels, or for a book that will simply make you love Jesus and his mission more, then take up and read.

Tony Merida, founding pastor, Imago Dei Church, Raleigh, NC;
Associate Professor of Preaching, Southeastern Baptist Theological Seminary

For a Christianity that has been lulled to sleep by a pleasant, self-help Messiah, this book is the awakening course-correction. In chapter after chapter, Steve Timmis brought me back to the sayings of Jesus I thought I'd made peace with and showed me afresh the tension his words were meant to create in the hearts of his hearers. I love his heart for clarity and his passion for the true Jesus to be known, regardless of how inconvenient he may be.

Matt Carter, Pastor of Preaching, Austin Stone Community Church;
coauthor, The Real Win

Steve Timmis has been used by God powerfully over the last decade to encourage us to think about the church in a way that is biblically faithful and tremendously helpful. In *I Wish Jesus Hadn't Said That* … Timmis once again serves us well by presenting to us the parts of Jesus' teachings that often get left out, but are imperative to our joy and gladness.

Matt Chandler, lead pastor, The Village Church, Dallas, Texas;
president, Acts 29 Church Planting Network

Steve Timmis's writing makes easy reading, without being shallow, as he treats some of Jesus' meaty sayings. Concise, relevant, and insightful.

Simon Guillebaud, missionary and author

Steve Timmis leads us with raw honesty through the challenges of some of the most radical, life-changing statements Jesus ever made. This is to be read with a notebook and pen, shared with friends, discussed in home groups, taught in discipleship classes, and preached from the pulpit. From new converts to those who have travelled a little further on the journey, here is a book that will not only nourish and challenge you to the core, but is also a brilliant, brilliant read.

This book shines light on ten things that Jesus said; ten things that blow cobwebs off compromise, cut like a razor into the very guts of our "faith in action," and dare us to build our lives on his terms.

This is a stimulating and inspiring book, and everyone will benefit from the lessons that are revealed ... I dare you to read, believe, and breathe it.

Thank you, Steve Timmis, for such a refreshingly honest read; you have left me challenged and determined to change.

I wish Steve hadn't shared this stuff ... but I'm really glad he did.

Mitch, evangelist, cofounder of Crown Jesus Ministries
and author of Snatched from the Fire

I found this book compulsive reading — I couldn't put it down!

Steve Timmis hits hard, but so truly and fairly. He kept reminding me of Jerry Bridges' book *Respectable Sins*, and I felt convicted in every chapter, but also encouraged to accept the challenge to change — and be changed — to become what Jesus wants me to be. Thank you, Steve!

Helen Roseveare, missionary and author

A profoundly challenging book. I was left reeling by these hard sayings of Jesus: first, when my mind acknowledged Jesus really had said what he said; secondly, when my heart began to wrestle with the implications; and thirdly, when my will cried to the Lord for help ... but then there were flickers of joy.

Rico Tice, All Souls Church, London, and Christianity Explored

FINDING JOY IN THE
INCONVENIENCE OF DISCIPLESHIP

I WISH JESUS HADN'T SAID THAT

STEVE TIMMIS

FOREWORD BY DANIEL L. AKIN

ZONDERVAN®

ZONDERVAN

I Wish Jesus Hadn't Said That
Copyright © 2013 by Steve Timmis

Originally published in the UK by Inter-Varsity Press
Norton Street, Nottingham NG7 3HR, England

This title is also available as a Zondervan ebook.
Visit www.zondervan.com/ebooks.

Requests for information should be addressed to:

Zondervan, *Grand Rapids, Michigan 49530*

Library of Congress Cataloging-in-Publication Data

Timmis, Steve, 1957–
    I wish Jesus hadn't said that : finding joy in the inconvenience of discipleship /
Steve Timmis.
      p.   cm.
    ISBN 978-0-310-51652-1 (softcover) — ISBN 978-0-310-51653-8 (ebook)
    1. Jesus Christ—Words. 2. Christian life. I. Title.
BT306.T56 2014
232.9'54—dc23   2013034283

Cover design: LUCAS Art and Design
Interior design: Ben Fetterley and Greg Johnson
Interior composition: Greg Johnson/Textbook Perfect

Printed in the United States of America

13 14 15 16 17 18 /DCI/ 22 21 20 19 18 17 16 15 14 13 12 11 10 9 8 7 6 5 4 3 2 1

✖

This book is dedicated to
a stepmother who was as loving and kind
as any mother could have been.

✖

Contents

FOREWORD

In Mark 1:22 the evangelist says of the people who listened to Jesus teach, "And they were astonished at his teaching, for he taught them as one who had authority and not as the scribes." Later, in John's gospel, after Jesus feeds the five thousand and preaches his great "Bread of Life" Sermon, we find the people once again "astonished" at his teaching. This time their astonishment is not positive. They are not applauding what they have just heard. Instead, they give his words a grade of F and walk away. Their evaluation is short and to the point: "This is a hard saying, who can listen to it?" (John 6:60).

If you read the gospels you will quickly find that Jesus said many hard and difficult things. Some of his words were hard for people to understand. They didn't grasp the meaning. But after his crucifixion and resurrection, the mist cleared a bit, and the obscured meaning behind his teaching emerged for us to see. There are other sayings of Jesus that fall into a different category, however. They are not hard to understand; their meaning is clear. These sayings are hard to *believe*, and they are hard to *obey*. When we hear Jesus say these things, we are tempted to object. We think, "You can't be serious, Jesus! You're kidding, right? No one can do that!"

I Wish Jesus Hadn't Said That is a wonderful short read that addresses ten of these hard and difficult sayings of Jesus. These are sayings that fall into the second category of difficulty, words that are difficult to obey and live out. They are radical calls to discipleship that can only be obeyed through the power of the gospel, by living moment to moment under the Lordship of King Jesus. These sayings can only be obeyed by those who deny themselves, take up their cross daily, and follow Jesus (Luke 9:23). Apart from our embrace of the crucified life, we will never grasp the import of these sayings, and we will not be able to live them out. The demands are too great. The bar is too high. The price is too costly. But the gospel has a way of changing things. It alters our worldview, transforms our perspective, and puts everything in a new light. Obedience is possible—even something to be enjoyed—when we obey in the power of the gospel.

Steve Timmis writes as a fellow disciple of King Jesus, someone who is in our corner and on our side. When I first met Steve, our hearts were knit and a new friendship was established with a brother in Christ. I appreciate Steve because he loves the gospel of our Lord Jesus Christ. Steve is vitally concerned that we not allow the disease of religiosity to infect the purity of the gospel and thereby pollute its message and render it sterile. We must guard the gospel at all cost.

Steve also loves the church. He has a passion for the body of Christ that is simply contagious. He has written this book to serve the Bride of Christ by challenging her to think rigorously in biblical and theological categories. To see the people of God *be* the people of God in their particular context and locale is a priority in Steve's ministry and one that is reflected beautifully in this book.

Finally, Steve loves the Great Commission, and he takes joy in playing his part to see the nations discipled and taught to obey all that the Lord has commanded. Steve longs to see those won to Christ discipled as devoted followers of King Jesus, who live daily the transformed lives of redeemed sinners. He is passionate about discipleship, as the subtitle makes evident.

Steve Timmis is a gift to the body of Christ for which I am thankful. He is possessed with an insight and wisdom that always challenges me, and he is blessed with a rare skill to take complex ideas and make them simple to understand. I pray that his tribe may multiply and increase! The church of the Lord Jesus needs more servants like him.

Daniel L. Akin
President, Southeastern Baptist Seminary
October 2013

ACKNOWLEDGMENTS

A huge thank you to Jen Baxter and Amy Tyson, whose editorial assistance was immense and invaluable. The book could not, and would not, have been written without you. Also, thank you to Eleanor Trotter, my IVP Editor. Your patience and encouragement were key to my persevering with the project. My thanks too to John Walley for stepping in at very short notice to help out with the final draft. Your comments were helpful, but your willingness was a lovely illustration of the truth I am trying to teach in this book.

Finally and especially, thank you to Janet, my long-suffering and faithful companion, without whom not only would this book not be what it is, but I would be far less of the man that I am. You have been the primary means of grace in my life, and I thank our Father for you daily.

PREFACE

Maybe it's because I am a cynical Englishman, but sometimes I think forewords can stray into cheesy territory. And given both the content and the style of this book, this is neither the time nor the place for cheesiness. Yet it is an opportunity to write one or two more personal things by way of, what you might call, acclimatization.

For the past sixteen years of my life and ministry, I have had the privilege of "doing church" differently. That's not my designation; it's how other people regularly describe it. The principal characteristic of this model or expression is a dual and equal commitment to the gospel Word and the gospel community, both of which I understand to be missional in character. Being immersed in this kind of church has profoundly shaped my understanding and experience of what it means to be a Christian. It has shown me that following Jesus is a beautifully all-encompassing reality. There is no area of my life that is not subject to God's saving, sovereign care. That includes my relationships, my affections, my emotions, my ambitions, my work, my leisure, my time, my money, my resources. You name it, and Jesus made it all, paid for it all, claims it all, and rules over it all. This is an altogether wonderful and liberating truth.

This book is born out of that experience and exposure. Which means that I am not writing as a theoretician, much less as some sort of spiritual guru sitting in splendid isolation, meditating on deep thoughts! I write this as a disciple, a fellow-follower of Christ, who knows first-hand the joys and frustration of what this means. I write as someone who has experienced profound joy and intense sadness, as it seems as though I am being saved again and again as I come to see my sin more clearly and experience the grace of God that comes to me in my Savior and Lord.

So thank you for reading this book. Or at least for intending to do so — I'm not making any assumptions. My prayer is that, as you read, you too will come to love Christ more through his Word, by the sovereign and supernatural work of his Holy Spirit.

Steve Timmis
January 2013

INTRODUCTION

Let's face it: sometimes being a follower of Jesus can be rather inconvenient. That admission may sound shocking, but we all know it to be true. So it's better that we get it out into the open. In fact, I'm going to go even further and say that following Jesus can be the proverbial "pain in the neck." It is this inconvenience that provides the backcloth to this book. But if some of the things Jesus said are indeed inconvenient, then Jesus himself is inconvenient. Some might say he is even something of a nuisance! He steps into our world and asks us for far more than a few songs sung in his honor on a Sunday morning or, for that matter, a few coins or even bills on the collection plate.

So yes, as Tom Hanks might say, "Houston, we have a problem," and the rest of the world has too, for that matter. But the problem isn't with Jesus; it lies with our contemporary culture. We are driven by a desire to secure our own happiness. We pursue the things we want in order to have status, to look and feel good. We pursue the relationships we want in order to have a fulfilling and satisfying life. We pursue health, wealth, and general prosperity. We mostly get along with people who like us, and see no reason to get along with those who don't. If someone steals from us or causes us physical harm, we eagerly see them convicted. We stand up for our rights. Those are the values that drive society. And Christians easily begin to see them as givens too. We buy into a way of seeing the world that is basically aligned to the world's ideas of what is necessary, reasonable, and worth having. This overarching view about things is our plausibility structure: we decide what is plausible and what makes sense, and what isn't or doesn't.

But each of the sayings of Jesus that we will consider together in this book turns our plausibility structure on its head. Each one shakes us up and reveals the ways in which, most of the time, we don't take Jesus seriously. At least, not at a functional level. What follows are often well-known sayings or stories of Jesus — we may even have read them countless times. But have we engaged with them on a level that prompts real action? Are we willing to have our perceptions of what is reasonable molded and shaped by our Savior, instead of by the world? If we call ourselves followers of Jesus, we must grapple at more than one level with what Jesus said this means.

The fact is that many people *do* follow Jesus, despite the inconvenience of his words and the demanding aspect of his presence. Something drives his followers to commit to him, to love him, to serve him, whatever the cost. There must be something compelling about Jesus for so many millions of people throughout history to have risked their safety and given their lives to follow him. There must be something that makes the suffering and sacrifice, the torture and even death, all worth it.

So while this book looks at sayings that cause me to sigh, "I wish Jesus hadn't said that …" — the refrain of each chapter is the final word: "But I'm really glad he did." I'm really glad Jesus *did* call me to follow him. I'm really glad Jesus *did* spell out just what it means to be his. I'm really glad Jesus *did* say all those things that invade my "private" world, break into my choices, and turn me and my lifestyle upside down. Because it is in that process of dislocation and disturbance that I discover Jesus to be everything I could ever need and my greatest delight in life. The joy of resting in his promises and walking with the Savior is far more significant and precious than any plan, dream, or ambition I would choose to pursue.

CHAPTER 1

Deny Yourself and Take Up Your Cross

Having been a Christian for a while now, I have learned many things about following Jesus. One of the most irritating discoveries has been the way that Jesus and his words intrude into our lives, force us out of our grooves, and mess around with our worlds. For all the talk about "gentle Jesus, meek and mild," he is actually a very disturbing person whose words are troubling words. I don't think I am on my own when I say that sometimes I just want to be left alone to get on with life as I prefer to live it. I just want to do my own thing. Of course, we don't want to ditch Jesus completely. We like being part of the Jesus club. He is always going to get our vote, and we're really glad that he died to save us from our sin. But though we nod our heads in recognition of, and thanks for, what he has done, we then carry on in our own sweet way.

But if all that we know about Jesus is true, then why and how can this be the case? Christians assert that Jesus is the Son of God, the One who died and rose again to purchase and liberate a lost and sinful people. We believe that Jesus is the One by whom, and through whom, all things were made, and that he is making all things new. We believe that he will return and reign in glory. We know that, when he lived on earth, he showed us glimpses of his future kingdom, as he healed the sick, raised the dead, calmed storms, loved sinners, and healed the broken-hearted. Why then are we disposed to dismissing this King so easily?

Searching for the Good Life

One of the benefits of my years of experience is that I have had plenty of time to ponder on the answer. During this time, I've concluded that it's a calculated decision. Allow me to explain to those of you who have not been on the road for quite as long as I have! We all want to live "the good life." We all want lives that are enjoyable and fulfilling. It's a strong desire, a passion, a drive, almost an instinct. Yes, we recognize that our lives can't always be good. But when they're not good, we're disappointed. And if that state of "not good" continues, and life consistently fails to live up to our expectations, we become despondent. Sometimes we get depressed because we're not living the life we wanted or expected. So what is this good life? It may not surprise you to discover that I've pondered long and hard about this one too! I think it is as simple as this: getting what we want. When we get what we want, we are happy and content. Until, that is, we want something else.

Obviously, having what we want will mean different things to different people. What do *you* imagine would give you "the good life"? It's not all that hard to answer. Just finish the sentence: "I would be really happy if I had …"

true love	health
a husband/wife	peace
children	comfort
a family	more time
friends	excitement and adventure

a job I liked	the perfect wave (water or hair!)
the right church	a manicure
wealth	*those* shoes
a nice house	season tickets

We're convinced that possessing *that thing* will lead us into the good life. At the very least, it will make us happier than we are today. So, mole-like, we scurry along in pursuit of our dreams, forever digging and tunneling. Isn't that what we're supposed to be doing, after all? We're content in our discontent, obediently reaching for the stars. We want it all, and we follow our desires (euphemistically called dreams). Often at any cost. Then Jesus comes along and stands in our way. He strides into *my* world and says, "Deny yourself, take up your cross and follow me." Exactly what is he talking about?

A Turning Point

The saying above occurred at a very significant juncture in Mark's account of the life, death, and resurrection of Jesus the Messiah. It was something of a turning point. Throughout Mark's account, "Who is this man?" is a recurring question that crops up in different forms in relation to Jesus' authority over demons, his claim to forgive sins, his ability to control the elements, heal the sick, feed the hungry, and raise the dead. Jesus knows he has caused quite a stir, and people are trying to figure him out. So he puts his disciples on the spot: what are they saying about me? They give a variety of speculative and fanciful answers, but then Jesus turns the full glare of the spotlight on his disciples and asks, "Who do *you* say I am?"

Peter comes right out with it, without so much as a second thought. This outspoken fisherman lands the catch in one swing: you are the Christ! By calling Jesus "the Christ," Peter was identifying Jesus as the one sent and empowered by God to fulfill hundreds of promises and satisfy the countless hopes and dreams of

God's people over the centuries. If Jesus was the Christ, then in him God was at work in a new and significant way. Something truly momentous had arrived. Not so much a once-in-a-lifetime event as a once-in-time event.

Peter and his friends understood this, which was why Jesus' following comments were so confusing and ridiculous. When they thought about "the Christ," they thought about victories, parades, and supremacy. They had visions of singing "Glory, glory, the Messiah" all the way down Jerusalem High Street. Instead of that, Jesus was saying that being the Messiah was all about misunderstanding, rejection, suffering, and death. No wonder Peter objected. But if a suffering Christ was bad news, then things were about to go downhill faster than Jack and Jill in their aborted water-collecting initiative.

"So you want to follow me, do you?" Jesus asks. Though this was spoken to a motley crowd in Palestine over 2,000 years ago, Jesus is addressing every aspiring follower since then. Up to this point everyone *did* want to follow him. Who wouldn't want to follow this wonder-working, sin-forgiving, life-restoring Master who strode authoritatively around the region? But then he drops the bombshell. He says, "Well, following me involves two essential elements: self-denial and cross-carrying."

Self-Denial

In an age of instant gratification, denial only exists as a river in Egypt. Everything in our culture says that we should pursue what we want. If you feel stuck in your marriage, leave it. If you want that promotion, go for it. If you don't want that baby, abort it. If you want that holiday, credit card it. Find your true desires and spend your life fulfilling them. You know you deserve it.

Enjoying the good things of this life that God gives us is not wrong. He has created us with unique personalities, gifts, and loves, and he wants us to enjoy him in those things. But our culture's obsession with getting what we want is the context that makes Jesus' words about denial sting. Not only are these words inconvenient for us, they're inconvenient for our friends too. What chance do we have of getting them interested in Jesus when Jesus is so hung up on self-denial?

What exactly is self-denial? It's "a total rejection of all self-worship and of every attempt to run your own life in pursuit of your own self-obsessed, self-glorifying dreams and ambitions." In other words, self-denial is when we say no to the human desire to rule our own lives. We stop trying to get for ourselves what we think we need or deserve. Self-denial is, instead, turning to worship the true God. We submit to his plans for our lives. We accept what he gives us with joy and contentment. We seek his glory above our own happiness. When the whisper of temptation says, "You know you want it," you respond with a loud and definitive, "No." When you hear those words, "You know you've earned it," you say again, simply, "No." When the seductive invitation says, "Because you're worth it," you firmly say, "No!"

But this call to self-denial is not a call to a life of abstinence and tedium. It is way more costly than that.

Cross-Carrying

The image of cross-carrying, though obscure to us, was one that those listening to Jesus would have been all too familiar with: a man struggling under the weight of a large piece of wood as he stumbled toward the site of his own execution. It meant suffering, torture, and death. Forget the religious ritual of Lent: to deny yourself is not saying no to chocolate for forty days. To deny yourself is to say yes to death.

Following Jesus ultimately means denying yourself the right to life itself. That's how total it is. Deciding to follow Jesus is saying,

"Jesus, I am going to follow you, and that means that I know that it's not my life any more. It's yours to do with as you please. By deciding to follow you, I am relinquishing all control and self-determination, and accepting that I may be called to suffer, be tortured, or even die for that decision."

It is interesting that this is not in the small print. The cost of following Jesus is written in large, bold letters for all to see. Jesus calls the whole crowd to hear these words, not just his disciples. This life-sacrificing self-denial isn't a special intensive course for those who are willing to give that little bit extra. This is discipleship at its most basic. This is the first time Jesus talks about discipleship, and this is the very first thing he says about it. And he says it to all of his prospective followers. This is the only kind of Christianity there is.

Consider pioneer missionary to Burma (now known as Myanmar), Adoniram Judson. In the course of his life as a missionary, he grieved the loss of two baby boys, his wife, his young daughter, his second wife, and three more children. But this suffering would not have surprised Adoniram. Here is an excerpt from the letter he wrote to his first wife's father, asking for his permission to marry her:

> I have now to ask whether you can consent to part with your daughter early next spring, to see her no more in this world? Whether you can consent to her departure to a heathen land, and her subjection to the hardships and sufferings of a missionary life? Whether you can consent to her exposure to the dangers of the ocean; to the fatal influence of the southern climate of India; to every kind of want and distress; to degradation, insult, persecution, and perhaps a violent death? Can you consent to all this, for the sake of him who left his heavenly home and died for her and for you; for the sake of perishing, immortal souls; for the sake of Zion and the glory of God? Can you consent to all this, in hope of soon meeting your daughter in the world of glory, with a crown of righteousness brightened

by the acclamations of praise which shall redound to her Savior from heathens saved, through her means, from eternal woe and despair? [1]

Is this what you signed up for when you decided to follow Jesus? That's the question we all must ask ourselves. If not, now's the time to admit it and get out while you're still alive. In the warmth of our living room or the comfort of a coffee shop or tea room, it's easy to sit back, relax, and say, "Yeah, I'm cool with that! If Jesus calls me to die for him and the gospel, so be it." But how do I know that, when push comes to shove, my life is expendable for the sake of Jesus and the gospel? We might say with all kinds of bravado how faithful we'd be … But how do we *know*?

Frankly, I don't think we can know for sure beforehand. But we can get a sense of our willingness to die for Jesus by what we're willing to endure or let go of now. I'll highlight a list of very pointed things. I hope that you will be offended by at least some of them!

If you're not prepared to miss your favorite TV show in order to visit the lonely old man next door, you can be certain you won't give up your life.

If you're not prepared to give up your bed to go and serve someone, you can be certain you won't give up your life.

If you're not prepared to pursue people who are different from you in order to be a blessing to them, you can be certain you won't give up your life.

If you're not prepared to give up a holiday abroad so you can give money to support someone in gospel ministry, you can be certain you won't give up your life.

If you're not prepared to miss out on a promotion so that you can free up time to stay around and plant churches, you can be certain you won't give up your life.

---

[1] Courtney Anderson, *To the Golden Shore: The Life of Adoniram Judson* (Zondervan, 1956), p. 83.

If you're not prepared to jeopardize a friendship, risk rejection, or ruin your street cred so that you can tell others about Jesus, you can be 100% sure that you won't give up your life.

In a sense, every time I say no to something I want, or no to something I regard as my right, or no to something I really enjoy, for the sake of Jesus and the gospel, then I am taking up my cross and dying to self. It's only as I learn to die to self in those little moments of daily existence that I will be prepared to give up my life in that big moment of crisis.

If we won't say no now, we will never, ever say no then. And if we won't give up our lives for Jesus, who gave up everything he had for us, then we might as well come clean and walk away right now.

The Really Really Good Life

But before we walk away, look at this: "If anyone is ashamed of me and my words in this adulterous and sinful generation, the Son of Man will be ashamed of them when he comes in his Father's glory with the holy angels" (Mark 8:38).

Jesus is fundamentally calling into question the calculated decision we referred to earlier when we were talking about our pursuit of "the good life." Jesus *is* calling us to make a calculated decision, but on the basis of eternity. Jesus is calling us to read-just our desires, calling our hearts to be captivated by the joy that will be ours when he returns "in his Father's glory with the holy angels." Which do we want more — our version of the good life or his? As C. S. Lewis so insightfully put it, by desiring and pursuing any of the things that we listed earlier more than we desire God, we are refusing a trip to the seaside because we want to stay and play in a slum:

> We are half-hearted creatures, fooling about with drink and sex
> and ambition when infinite joy is offered us, like an ignorant
> child who wants to go on making mud pies in a slum because

he cannot imagine what is meant by the offer of a holiday at the sea. We are far too easily pleased.[2]

We're exchanging the glory of the pounding surf and endless sand for playing around in a muddy puddle. But Jesus is calling us to live in the light of that moment when the kingdom of God will come in all of its breathtaking and staggering glory.

That is life in all its fullness. *That* is the life to be lived, loved, and longed for! In that very moment, when we see God in all of his triune glory as Father, Son, and Holy Spirit, we will know what life was meant to be. When the crucified, risen, glorified Jesus is seen by all, and we look upon the nail-prints in his hands and feet, and the spear mark in his side — at that very moment we will know, for the very first time, what it really means to be alive. In one exquisite and awesome instant, we will say, this is it — this is everything my heart has ever craved! This is everything I have ever been looking for — everything I have ever truly wanted is *now*!

In *The Problem of Pain*, C. S. Lewis writes, "There have been times when I think we do not desire heaven; but more often I find myself wondering whether, in our heart of hearts, we have ever desired anything else."[3] Those things we demand in order to bring us the good life will disappoint us. Often we want things that are objectively good, like health, marriage, family, peace, and satisfaction. But when we demand these things in order to feel happy, we are bound to be disappointed. They cannot live up to our longing, because our longing is for heaven. It can only be satisfied by Christ Jesus and fulfilled in our heavenly home.

All the things that have ever deeply possessed your soul have been but hints of it — tantalizing glimpses, promises never quite fulfilled, echoes that died away just as they caught your ear. But if it should really become manifest — if there ever

---

[2] C. S. Lewis, *The Weight of Glory* (HarperCollins, 2001), p. 26.
[3] C. S. Lewis, *The Problem of Pain* (Centenary Press, 1941), p. 133.

came an echo that did not die away but swelled into the sound itself — you would know it. Beyond all possibility of doubt you would say "Here at last is the thing I was made for."[4]

So whatever we say no to now — including life itself — is a small price to pay. In that moment of glory, when it all makes sense and it all comes together, just think how sordid and shoddy that bed, holiday, promotion, snobbery, friendship, or street cred is going to look. They matter so much to us now, but Jesus promises us that they will mean nothing at all then. And those good longings which were never fulfilled: the saying goodbye to family and friends for the sake of the gospel, the willingness to forego our dream home in the countryside or the family life we've always imagined, in order to follow Jesus ... all of these things *then* will take on the glorious richness of lives lived in submission to our Lord and refined by his loving hand. "In all this you greatly rejoice," says Peter who was later martyred, "though now for a little while you may have had to suffer grief in all kinds of trials. These have come so that the proven genuineness of your faith — of greater worth than gold, which perishes even though refined by fire — may result in praise, glory and honor when Jesus Christ is revealed" (1 Peter 1:6 – 7).

Do I Still Wish Jesus Hadn't Said That?

Yes, Jesus calls us to give up our ambitions and our petty pursuit of all those trinkets we so value. He calls us to submit the genuinely good things, even our lives, to him. But that call isn't so that we live an impoverished, stingy and depressing life now. We can live the life we were always made to live. And *that* is the really really good life. Jesus himself is the source of all joy, all peace, all hope, all love, all power, and all beauty. Giving up everything to gain him is gaining everything.

---

[4] Ibid., p. 134.

I can't cut it out of my Bible. Jesus definitely said, "If anyone would follow me, let him deny himself, take up his cross and follow me." Do I still wish Jesus hadn't said that? Not at all. In fact, I am really glad he did!

CHAPTER 2

Love Your Enemies

This is a double-take moment. Or one of those awkward moments when someone says something that, when you first hear it, causes you to laugh, only to realize that it was in fact a serious comment.

Love your enemies? Turn the other cheek? Give your jumper and your coat? You have got to be kidding, Jesus! But apparently not. So let's look at what he actually said, in order to see how we can make sense of such apparent absurdity.

> But I say to you who hear, Love your enemies, do good to those who hate you, bless those who curse you, pray for those who abuse you. To one who strikes you on the cheek, offer the other also, and from one who takes away your cloak do not withhold your tunic either. Give to everyone who begs from you, and from one who takes away your goods do not demand them back. And as you wish that others would do to you, do so to them. If you love those who love you, what benefit is that to you? For even sinners love those who love them. And if you do good to those who do good to you, what benefit is that to you? For even sinners do the same. And if you lend to those from whom you expect to receive, what credit is that to you? Even

*sinners lend to sinners, to get back the same amount. But love your
enemies, and do good, and lend, expecting nothing in return, and
your reward will be great, and you will be sons of the Most High, for
he is kind to the ungrateful and the evil. Be merciful, even as your
Father is merciful. (Luke 6:27 – 36 ESV)*

I am going to be honest with you. I don't want to love my
enemies. In my worst moments, I want to hurt them, gossip about
them, undermine them, and generally make them pay. In my better moments, I simply want to ignore, sideline, and ostracize them.
If I am not in a position to retaliate, I can at least wait until someone or something else makes sure my enemy gets their comeup-
pance. Then I can sit and gloat. I can enjoy the warm satisfaction
of knowing that they finally got what they deserved.

But Jesus says that none of that behavior is an option for a follower of his. Deeper than that, none of those desires is an option
for a follower of his. His command is that we love our enemies. We
simply cannot follow Jesus and hate others — even "others" who
hate us. It's like trying to mix oil and water, or pour a gallon into a
pint pot. No matter how hard you try, it just won't happen. More
significantly, it is not *meant* to happen.

Who Are My Enemies?

Perhaps if we get to grips with what Jesus actually meant, we will
be able to see that it's not so bad after all. A little work here might
save a lot of disappointment later.

My enemy is someone who hates, curses, and abuses me. Look
at the last part of verse 27 and verse 28: "... do good to those who
hate you, bless those who curse you, pray for those who abuse
you." Jesus doesn't say why they view me as their enemy; he doesn't
explain if it is because I have done something I should not have
done, or not done something I should have done. He simply iden-
tifies them by their attitude toward me.

Can you see the significance of that? Followers of Jesus should not have enemies, in the sense that they should not regard others as enemies; they should simply recognize when they are the enemies of others.

Suddenly I am caught like a rabbit in a set of headlights. I know, deep down, that I do view others as my enemy: I do hate, curse, and mistreat others. Not in any crude, socially, or even spiritually unacceptable way, but quietly, in the secrecy of my own heart. When someone regards me with disdain, they effectively become my enemy. I don't like them anymore. I'll pretend I don't see them sitting across the room in Starbucks. If I happen to notice that they've spilled their sugar-free vanilla latte all over the floor, I will probably smile.

Why? Because my pride is hurt. I cannot understand why they don't like me, or how they can so misunderstand me. How can they possibly do what they are doing to me? And when my pride is wounded, I want to retaliate and lash out. But Jesus says it should not be that way. He says I will have enemies, of course, in the sense that I will have people who hate, curse, and mistreat me. But I am not to hate, curse, or mistreat anyone else.

Surely Not?

It would at least be bearable if we could stop here. I can live with not hating, cursing, or mistreating these people. But sadly, Jesus isn't content with merely the absence of negatives.

Jesus says our response should be shaped by the attitudes and actions directed toward us by those who hate us, but not in any "like-for-like" sense. (We need to be sure we understand what Jesus said here, because, to put it mildly, it is all rather counter-intuitive!)

If your enemy hits you on one cheek, then give them the other one too.

If someone takes your coat, then let them take your sweater as well.

Whatever they demand, give it to them and do not pursue them to retrieve it.

Jesus was speaking into a specific cultural situation, using contemporary illustrations to make his point clear. Each of the three scenarios would therefore have been familiar and common. Israel was an occupied territory, and an occupying force is not going to observe all the social niceties of "please" and "thank you." The Romans had a sense of right that accompanied their all-too-obvious show of might. A little well-placed force every now and again reminded people of their rightful place in the "empire."

Reading these examples and knowing something of the context they were spoken into, I find myself wanting to respond with one of those "you-cannot-be-serious" rants! "Love your enemies" just doesn't make any sense. If we follow what Jesus said, we are going to end up as doormats, which, let's face it, is not a very appealing prospect and certainly a hard sell to my friends. In fact, everything in me screams, "No!" It flies in the face of natural justice. It repulses my well-developed instinct for retaliation and self-protection. It is the kind of ethic that sounds fine in the safety of our living rooms, but out there, on the cold, hard streets of the real world?

If anyone else had said this, we could ignore them. It is only because these words come from the lips of Jesus that we cannot do so. We ignore them at our peril, and to our eternal loss.

So what exactly is Jesus getting at?

First, my primary response to those who see themselves as my enemy is to do good to them, to bless them, and to pray for them.

Imagine you live in a country where it is illegal to be a Christian. Word gets out that you follow Jesus, and you face daily threats and persecution from your next-door neighbors. What would you do? Would you not try to keep your head down and make very sure you were never outside at the same time? Might you just allow bitterness to linger in your heart, wishing they would leave you alone and mind their own business?

Or imagine that you are walking along a snowy street, when you slip on ice and fall. Some nearby teenagers begin laughing and throwing snowballs at you. What would you do? Would you stand up indignantly and shout some abuse? Or simply get to your feet, recover your dignity and tentatively proceed on your way, muttering under your breath about jerks and louts? Would you want the best for them in your heart, or would you be secretly hoping that they would sustain some kind of snow-related injury?

Left to our own devices, we will resent anyone who wounds or accuses us. Yet here is Jesus, telling us to do them good. He says we must not just endure our enemies, but actively seek to bless them. We must not just tolerate those who would hurt us, but pray for their good. Which I suspect means that muttering "hello" in Starbucks and grudgingly wiping up the spilt latte is not enough. If that was all that was required, then I would be first in line with a paper towel, before sitting back, smugly content in my own righteousness.

The Golden Rule

Just when you think it's safe to go back into the water, Jesus' words come with a bite sharper than Jaws after a diet. He widens the scope of his command and ups the ante by showing that much more is required of us than merely outward behavior. But what does that kind of truly loving behavior look like in our day-to-day lives?

Think for a moment of what you want from others. Obviously, you do not want them slapping, cursing, and mistreating you. But more than that, you want people to be interested in your good and concerned about your happiness. You want others to please and serve you, care about you always, help you whenever, and want the best for you in any and every situation. Well, this is how Jesus calls me to treat others, especially when they misuse and abuse me. In every situation, my response to them should be <u>defined by their good, not my own.</u>

Think again about those two scenarios: persecution from neighbors and anti-social behavior from the local youth. Can you imagine responding to those "enemies" by not merely avoiding them, but actively seeking to do them good? Can you imagine how radically striking it would be to shower blessings upon them and to seek to love the very people who have been making your life miserable? That kind of response would be both stunning and inexplicable. Jesus calls us to <u>"love"</u> and <u>"do good."</u> Which means that any action or response on our part is motivated by love (not malice) and <u>actively seeks their good</u> (not our indulgence). This is so, so important. To do them good is to do that which will most benefit them, to reflect God's character and imitate his actions. So good has a contextual shape. It is personal and tailor-made. Loving and doing good to a sociopath is going to look very different from how we love and do good to a people-pleaser. But the call to love stands in both cases.

Jesus is calling us to radically distinct behavior that challenges people at an instinctive level. In each of the situations Jesus presents, <u>we are called to do what would least be expected.</u> It's not only "do not hit back," but "present the other cheek." It's not just "let him take your cloak," but "let him have your tunic too." Jesus does not tell us just to "give to everyone who asks," but commands that we "don't demand back what has been taken"!

This is not mere acquiescence or compliance. This radical enemy love is a call to actively engage in behavior that will challenge what people have done, because it asks fundamental questions about life and human identity. Here's what I mean.

A Different Model

A slap on the cheek is not so much an act of violence as an insult. If someone wants to hurt you physically, they will hit you with a clenched fist, rather than slap you with an open hand. By slapping you, they are trying to demean and dismiss you. By offering the other cheek, you are not just giving in to the physical violence of a bully; you are showing indifference to the insult. By letting someone take your tunic as well as your cloak, you are not being a wimp; you are showing outrageous generosity. By not demanding back what has been taken, you are not simply lying down and playing dead; you are showing that life is not defined by what you have.

Here is a completely different model of what it means to be human. Those things that matter so much to everyone else — reputation, rights, and possessions — actually mean so little to you.

Although I have not had to endure any of these offenses, I have had people say critical and hurtful things about me, attempting to damage my reputation. I have had people borrow something precious that belonged to me and abuse it. There are people who are theologically very different from me who regard my convictions as unhelpful and even dangerous. According to Jesus, none of these individuals is my enemy. I have no need to defend my name, demand restitution, or speak critically and demeaningly of others. I am called to love and bless each and every one of them.

But Why?

None of this should surprise us, because that was how it was with Jesus. He was slapped and did not retaliate. He was stripped bare and did not complain. Throughout his time on earth, he gave life and blessing to anyone who asked of him, no matter how much they were using and abusing him. And in the end, he had everything taken from him and he didn't demand it back.

In this call to love even our enemies, Jesus is calling us to be as he was and to live the life he lived. He is calling us to be human, as he was human. Not loving our enemies and not seeking their good is disobedience. But it is so much more than that. It is being less than God made us to be. If Jesus is our definition of true humanity, then not loving our enemies is being subhuman.

I have thought about the "why" question a great deal, and reckon it comes down to this: if we don't behave in this way, we are acting as though Jesus never existed!

See what Jesus himself says:

> *If you love those who love you, what benefit is that to you? For even sinners love those who love them. And if you do good to those who do good to you, what benefit is that to you? For even sinners do the same. And if you lend to those from whom you expect to receive, what credit is that to you? Even sinners lend to sinners, to get back the same amount. But love your enemies, and do good, and lend, expecting nothing in return, and your reward will be great, and you will be sons of the Most High, for he is kind to the ungrateful and the evil. Be merciful, even as your Father is merciful. (Luke 6:32 – 36 ESV)*

Our usual behavior of loving those who love us is a universal response. Even dogs know when people like them, and respond to affection by licking the hand that has been patting them. But Jesus intends for his people to be beautifully distinct in a world where hating those who hate you is not only acceptable, but also expected.

But where this is at its most beautiful and most hopeful is in the final phrase: "Be merciful, even as your Father is merciful." It is so easy for us to get intimidated by the commands and requirements we find in the Bible. Jesus tells me to love my enemies, and because it's him telling me, I want to obey. But then I am overwhelmed by the weight of that command, in danger of being crushed by the expectations. Even the encouragement to be like Jesus, though well-meant, threatens to suffocate me. But remember this: neither Jesus nor anyone else in the Bible is asking us to do what we cannot do; they are always encouraging us to be who we are. I am a child of God. The call to obedience is not so much to "imitate Christ" as to enjoy being "in Christ." It is because I am united to Christ the Son that I am a son of God, and it is as a child of my Father that I am to be merciful.

Our Father wants his children to march to a different drum, dance to a different beat and sing an altogether different song from everyone else. Loving our enemies Jesus' way makes us a radically and starkly different kind of people, not only in our outward actions, but also in the values those actions express.

Loving our enemies means ...

- we are a people for whom status, reputation, possessions, and rights have no hold.
- we have been changed to the very core of our being, rather than merely modified at the margins of our existence.

Do you want to be like everyone else? Do you really want to live life with Jesus as your "bit on the side"? Do you want to behave as though what Jesus was and did has no substantial bearing upon how you live your life and the kind of person you are? If we know anything at all about King Jesus, of course we don't! So why do we act as if Jesus' words don't matter?

Part of our problem is being besotted with the immediate and the tangible. Like Freddie Mercury of the rock group Queen, we want it all and we want it now. The problem with our pursuit of status, reputation, possessions, and rights is that it is insatiable. Whatever we get can never be good or great enough to quench our need. In fact, those desires are, at heart, a longing for something more. We attempt to satiate our longing for the transcendent with the mundane, which is why we are always left dissatisfied and disappointed. Only Jesus gives true satisfaction, which is why he offers us the freedom to be absolutely joyful when we have nothing of value in the world's eyes. Jesus died and rose again to give us the good life. We can risk everything, because we already have everything in him.

But How?

I have to confess that I conceded the argument about loving our enemies a long time ago. Good as I am at debating, I know I am no match for Jesus. Which means that the "how" question is one I have been yearning to ask since the beginning. The answer is breathtaking.

> But love your enemies, and do good, and lend, expecting nothing in return, and your reward will be great, and you will be sons of the Most High, for he is kind to the ungrateful and the evil. Be merciful, even as your Father is merciful. (vv. 35 – 36 ESV)

These verses hold two crucial answers to the "how" question.

1. Not Yet

First, we are to live for the age to come ("your reward will be great"), as children of our heavenly Father ("you will be sons of the Most High").

If the gospel is true and Jesus is who he claimed to be, then we can be sure of this one thing: there will come a moment when time ends and we will see the truth in all of its glorious and spectacular clarity. At that moment our attraction to status, reputation, possessions, and rights will look as cheap and nasty and futile as it really is.

We are to live in the light of our reward to come: eternity with our Lord, who will be honored and adored for his glorious grace, which was sufficient to transform sinners like us into true humans after the image of his Son. Eternity shows us up for what we truly are. If we are children of the living God, then eternity will reveal that for all to see. Our reward will be to bask for eternity in Jesus' glory and live renewed lives.

2. Now

We are to respond with active mercy to the active mercy we have received: "Be merciful, even as your Father is merciful." The call of Jesus is to live that life of fresh, active mercy now. Because as we, when lost in the mire of our selfishness, cruelty, and rebellion, received his mercy, we are to extend mercy to those who don't deserve it.

So revisit the great truths of the gospel often. Remind yourself and others of who Christ is and what he has done for you. Massage the message of the cross into your heart at every opportunity and celebrate what God has done for us in Christ. Being conscious of his mercy will dispose us to being merciful. We love our enemies because it was while we were still sinners that Christ died for us. As we show mercy to others, we reflect the mercy of our Father which has been lavished on us.

In a scene in Shakespeare's *The Merchant of Venice*, Portia, in the guise of a lawyer, tries to convince the wronged Shylock to grant mercy and allow Antonio to keep his pound of flesh:

> The quality of mercy is not strain'd,
> It droppeth as the gentle rain from heaven
> Upon the place beneath: it is twice blest;
> It blesseth him that gives and him that takes: ...
> And earthly power doth then show likest God's
> When mercy seasons justice ...
> That, in the course of justice, none of us
> Should see salvation: we do pray for mercy;
> And that same prayer doth teach us all to render
> The deeds of mercy.

I know my instinct is to refuse this approach to life, but on those occasions when I've taken it to heart, I am always shocked by the difference it makes. I think of Justin (not his real name), who betrayed our friendship and tried to damage my reputation. I was hurt and confused, angry and bitter. I nurtured those emotions for some time and, every time I thought about the betrayal, I felt a fresh surge of bitterness. But the Holy Spirit brought Jesus' words to my mind and convicted me of the self-righteousness that was bound up in my resentment. I reflected on my own all-too-frequent betrayal of the Lord in my sin. My heart was broken. I confessed my sin and asked for grace so that I could also forgive. I still grieve the loss of a friendship, but I know that my heart is free from bitterness and hurt, and I can pray for my brother to prosper and flourish.

Do I Still Wish Jesus Hadn't Said That?

"Love your enemies," Jesus said. Yes, at times I wish he hadn't said that. But in truth, I am so very glad he did.

CHAPTER 3

Not Seven Times, but Seventy-Seven Times

Like any husband, Uncle John sometimes made mistakes. Sometimes silly mistakes. Very silly mistakes. When he did, Aunty Mary would point out his error. Eventually, Uncle John would apologize and they would make up. Much to Uncle John's annoyance, Aunty Mary would, not infrequently, remind him of his misdemeanors. On one occasion, after such a reminder, he asked her why she had brought it up again when at the time she had said she would "forgive and forget." "I just don't want you to forget that I've forgiven and forgotten," she replied.

I wonder if Aunty Mary was familiar with this saying of Jesus? If she was, then it seems she was sticking to the letter of the law, rather than abiding by the spirit of it!

> *Peter came to Jesus and asked, "Lord, how many times shall I forgive my brother or sister who sins against me? Up to seven times?"*
>
> *Jesus answered, "I tell you, not seven times, but seventy-seven times." (Matthew 18:21–22)*

I quite like the idea of forgiveness. I suspect we all do. So, at least at one level, I'm not upset about Jesus commending it. After all, forgiveness has such a good vibe — like love, hope, and marshmallows. I especially like forgiveness when I receive it. Even the ludicrously high "seventy-seven times" or "seventy times seven" sounds an excellent idea when I am the one who has messed up.

But once I'm over the feel-good factor of the word, I realize that this statement of Jesus places me in an awkward situation. It means that, if I am serious about following Jesus, I have to forgive, forgive, and forgive again. And that is just for starters. Which is not only tedious, but somewhat inconvenient. Is Jesus *really* saying that, if someone keeps stabbing me in the back, I have to keep forgiving them? It would seem so. At least at face value. But that is outrageous. Maybe Jesus' requirement for us to forgive those who sin against us refers only to relatively minor sins: they failed to give back the DVD they borrowed; they arrived six minutes late for the meal; they didn't reply to the text I sent five minutes ago? I am probably gracious enough to forgive those "sins," even if they all happen in the same day, by the same person. Probably.

But Jesus does not make such distinctions. Someone who can forgive those who are torturing and executing him clearly has a very high view of forgiveness (Luke 23:34). Yet what he says about unlimited forgiveness does not sit well with my desire to keep a record of wrongs. So we're going to consider just how serious Jesus was in his instruction to forgive, apparently ad infinitum.

Forgiveness: The General versus the Jesus View

Forgiveness isn't just a Christian phenomenon. In recent years, psychologists have done quite a bit of research into forgiveness, with tests and studies to figure out our attitudes. They have found that people who forgive report an improved quality of relationships and a higher commitment to relationships than those who refuse to forgive. The findings of a specific study showed that forgiveness happens when our desires change, so that we actually want to forgive.[5]

Other studies have shown that forgiveness is actually good for our health. *Psychological Science* reported that one study asked seventy undergraduates to think about a time when they were treated badly by someone. The participants then practiced either forgiving the person who had hurt them, or not forgiving. The results showed that a sustained pattern of unforgiveness over time can result in poorer health.[6]

So experts say that forgiveness is good for us. Though I suspect we didn't need a survey to tell us that. We all know something of the tension and anxiety we experience when we harbor grudges. It's what the experts do not tell us that is the critical issue. Namely, how we can become those who want to forgive. How do we experience that transformation of our desires, so that we no longer want to hurt or exclude those who wrong us, but forgive them instead? The only answer secular psychology can give is sheer determination, based on an ability to rise above our natural instinct for revenge and hatred. But I know one thing for certain: if a change in my desires is required for me to forgive, then I am exposed and without hope, because I am unable to control what my heart truly wants.

Jesus calls us to a forgiveness that knows no bounds and extends to the cruelest oppressor. His view of forgiveness is not dependent upon whether the person is sorry, or whether they have tried to change their ways. Yes, I know this is what many people

---

[5] Adam Cohen, "Research on the Science of Forgiveness: An Annotated Bibliography," October 1, 2004, http://greatergood.berkeley.edu/article/item/the_science_of_forgiveness_an_annotated _bibliography (accessed March 30, 2012).
[6] Ibid.

argue, saying that, in the gospel, God requires confession and repentance before he grants forgiveness. The problem with this view is that, unintentionally, it underplays the work of the Holy Spirit. We need him to work in order for us to repent (2 Timothy 2:25). The faith needed to believe the gospel is itself a gift from God (Ephesians 2:8). But clearly, we don't have divine ability in our dealings with others. So what option do we have left to us? Pray that God will grant them repentance and then harbor a grudge against them? Or keep a record of their wrong until he does? That doesn't seem to track with what Jesus is saying here at all. Jesus' version of forgiveness is resilient, strong, and supernaturally powerful. And one that is far more compelling and attractive than ours.

In his book, *Rumors of Another World*, Philip Yancey tells of a very disturbing event that took place during the Truth and Reconciliation hearings in South Africa in the days immediately after the ending of apartheid:

> At one hearing, a policeman named van de Broek recounted an incident when he and other officers shot an eighteen-year-old boy and burned the body, turning it on the fire like a piece of barbecue meat in order to destroy the evidence. Eight years later van de Broek returned to the same house and seized the boy's father. The wife was forced to watch as policemen bound her husband on a woodpile, poured gasoline over his body, and ignited it. The courtroom grew hushed as the elderly woman who had lost first her son and then her husband was given a chance to respond. "What do you want from Mr. van de Broek?" the judge asked.[7]

What do you think the woman said? What would you have said?

---

[7] Philip Yancey, *Rumors of Another World: What on Earth Are We Missing?* (Zondervan, 2003), p. 223.

Compassion, Retribution, and Justice

The first thing to recognize is that the question: "How many times shall I forgive?" is not totally naïve. Peter is showing what is in his heart: "I know you've told us to forgive, Lord, and I want to obey, but I also want to know how far I should go." His question is essentially: "When is it legitimate for me to stop?" This is the question of a legalist, and it is one that is not far from all of our minds. If forgiveness is mandatory, then we want to do what we must, but strictly no more. For Peter, forgiving someone seven times was the epitome of grace. It was, after all, more than twice what most rabbis were advocating.

But Jesus deconstructs Peter's question. He exposes its folly, showing that forgiveness is not a question of mathematics, but a matter of the heart. To demonstrate this principle, Jesus tells a story in which there are three significant scenes:

A high-ranking servant owes his king an outrageous amount of money, and cannot afford to pay it back. The amount of the debt is ludicrously large, so big that it would be obvious to Jesus' listeners that the servant could never pay it back. At first, the king acts reasonably: he orders that the servant, with his wife, children, and all of their possessions, be sold as payment. The desperate servant prostrates himself before the king, pleading with him, throwing himself upon his mercy. And then the king does far more than the servant dares to hope for. The servant is begging for more time to pay, but the king cancels the debt entirely. The king would have known that the debt could never be repaid. The only options here are judgment or grace. The king chooses grace. Outrageous grace.

It is difficult to imagine how the story should go after this. This seems to be the climax of the narrative, and anything else is going to be disappointing. But the primary point of this particular story is not the outrageous grace of the king, but the deep and profound insensitivity to grace on the part of the servant. He leaves the presence of the king without so much as a thank-you, and immediately meets a fellow servant who owes him a hundred denarii. That detail is vital. It tells us that the first servant owed the king around 600,000 times more than his fellow servant owed him. Yet he now grabs his fellow servant by the neck, choking him and demanding payment. This scene deliberately re-enacts the first exchange with the king. There are similar phrases and imagery. Both servants use, virtually word for word, the same plea: "Be patient with me, and I will pay you back." But where the king acted in compassion, the servant acts in retribution: he refuses to listen and walks away, ordering the second servant to be thrown into prison until he can pay.

The first servant behaves as though he has neither knowledge nor experience of grace, despite his own debt being cancelled. When the king hears about this turn of events, he acts appropriately. He calls the "evil" servant back, angry that he who had been shown such mercy did not then show mercy to others. The king turns him over to the jailers to be punished until he can pay back all he owes.

Grace Produces Grace

Let's go back for a moment to Peter's question. I don't know about you, but I find it an altogether reasonable question. Peter would have expected Jesus to say something like, "Seven times should do it," or maybe, if he is feeling particularly generous, twelve times. But Jesus replies with this ridiculously high "seventy times seven." Peter, along with everyone else listening in, would have been shocked. Which is why Jesus tells his story, because it is a snapshot of our hearts.

It is an immutable law of spiritual dynamics that a personal experience of grace will produce more grace. That first servant walked out of the king's presence with nothing more than a feeling of relief that he was not going to prison. He showed no sense of amazement at the kindness of his master. He felt no desire to act in grace toward his fellow servant because he had no sense of the stunning grace he had just experienced.

Like that first servant, our own willingness to forgive is the surest indicator of our knowledge and experience of forgiveness. This is what Jesus said in what we call the Lord's Prayer: "For if you forgive other people when they sin against you, your heavenly Father will also forgive you, But if you do not forgive others their sins, your Father will not forgive your sins" (Matthew 6:14 – 15). Jesus is not saying that our forgiveness is earned by our willingness to forgive others. Rather, this is a shocking way of making a vital point: you have not enjoyed God's unmerited forgiveness if you are unable or unwilling to respond in kind toward others.

In my more transparent moments, I am prepared to admit that the principal reason why I wish Jesus hadn't said that I need to forgive someone "seventy times seven" is that I have no real sense of my own sin. I prefer to ignore the deep darkness of my own heart. And don't we all choose to excuse, explain, condone, and reason away our own actions, so that we don't feel such a need for forgiveness ourselves? But how can we enjoy God's lavish forgiveness if we don't think we need it? A reluctance to forgive someone reveals our self-preoccupied, self-righteous heart. We are angry about the wrongs done against us, as if we ourselves are innocent of wrongdoing. In my world, I am always the victim. Almost certainly I will be a stoical, even noble, victim — but I am a victim nonetheless.

Yet the gospel tells us that we have been forgiven so much more than we can begin to imagine. Do we really believe that our own personal sin against God is far more appalling and offensive than any sin anyone could ever commit against us? Dare we look at the ugly pride that is our personal rebellion against God, without excuse or attempt at justification?

Sin Matters

I am not minimizing, much less excusing, the wrong actions of others. People do commit horrendous acts that leave lifelong scars. You may be someone struggling to forgive verbal, physical, emotional, or sexual abuse, adultery, racial discrimination or some other form of societal or personal injustice. Recipients of these and other sins *are* victims. But we must not buy the lie that says that, in forgiving someone who has committed a heinous crime against me, I am making light of that sin. Nothing could be farther from the truth. Forgiveness is only possible because God has both declared and demonstrated that sin is eternally significant. Far from minimizing wrong, forgiveness names it for what it principally is: an act of treason against God that ultimately only he can deal with. Because sin matters, sin must be punished. God will deal with those who have hurt us, and he will do so in his own scrupulously wise and effective way.

But regardless of sin done against us, we all must stand before our Lord. We all must recognize the magnitude of what we have done against him in refusing to love, with all our being, the God who made, loved, and gave himself for us. Every lie, every act of violence, every refusal to love and honor others must face the judgment of a holy God. It is only as I have a true and tender sense of the magnitude of the gospel that I will find my heart soft toward others. Refusing to forgive, holding a grudge, wallowing in bitterness are all indicators of a heart that is indifferent to the Savior who suffered and died for me. Yes, there is a cost. Someone always has to pay for sin. For those who trust in him, that someone was Jesus. The Judge himself is judged for us, and the penalty he demands, he pays.

Yet it is no surprise that we struggle to forgive those who wound us. It offends our sense of justice. How can it be right to bear the weight not only of being sinned against, but also seeing our oppressor go unpunished? Both justice and vengeance set the record straight. They act as equalizers, resolving the moral deficit caused by the offense. But the words of Jesus contain no exception clause, no alternative.

So what can we do — how can we change? How do we embrace the freedom of forgiveness with hearts that continue to forgive others, time and again?

Gobsmacked by Grace

We must go to the God and Father of the Lord Jesus Christ for forgiveness. Ask him to show you, by his Spirit, the reality of your sin, so that you grieve and become broken-hearted over it. Then rejoice in the astounding truth that, while you were stuck in weakness and powerless in sin, God reached down and rescued you. He didn't wait until you got your act together, tried harder, smiled more, or sinned less. Like using bare hands to pick a soiled cloth out of stagnant water, he scooped you out of the slime of your rebellion against him. Meditate deeply on the great kindness of your Savior. Then, having experienced his unbelievable grace, you will be amazed at your desire and capacity to act in unbelievable grace toward others.

It is because of the magnificent, pivotal, defining work of Jesus on the cross, and only because of it, that I can forgive someone when they sin against me. Seventy times seven if necessary. When I refuse to forgive, I am saying that the cross is not adequate; Christ's death is not sufficient. The gospel declares that all sin has to be paid for and all sin will be paid for. This payment occurs at either the cross or the throne of judgment. So when I forgive others, I am refusing to exact a double payment. I am saying that I can trust God not only with my sin, but also with the sin done against me. And that, I can tell you, is good news indeed.

Consider, for a moment, the alternatives. The one that immediately springs to mind is unforgiveness, and that is clearly an option. And, at times, a very attractive option too. But is it really? And where does it leave us? Where does it leave the offender? How does it impact on the situation or resolve the issue? One thing I know for certain is that I am utterly incapable of changing anything in the past. The past may have enduring and painful repercussions, but I can never revisit it, no matter how much I want to. But we can do something about the present, and therefore the future. We can ask our kind and generous Father for sufficient grace to be who he calls and equips us to be as his children. We can live in the light of the forgiveness that is ours in Christ. As the forgiven, we can be the forgivers, since forgiveness is integral to our identity as beneficiaries of God's grace that comes to us in Christ. So, in forgiving, we are being no more and no less than who we are. As with every other "gospel requirement," it is always about being who we are becoming in Christ. As such, it is neither onerous nor crushing.

But enough of the rhetoric! What does this actually look like in practice?

Tom and June discovered that their sixteen-year-old daughter had been sexually abused by a young man in their church eight years earlier. She was now a Christian and didn't want professional counseling. It wasn't that she was opposed to it, simply that she didn't see the need for it. She had forgiven the man, and insisted that they had to do so too. She wanted two things from her parents: prayer for her heart to stay soft, so that bitterness and hatred wouldn't creep up on her, and wisdom to know whether or not she should go to the police, not out of vengeance, nor even a desire for justice, but simply because, if he had done things to her, he could be doing them to others too. And it was loving neither to him nor to them to let it continue.

❈ ❈ ❈

Jayne's mother had left her father when Jayne was approaching adolescence. Her mother had told her how much she loved her and that, although she needed to go, she would always keep in contact regularly. Over the years, Jayne realized that those words were empty indeed. Her mother didn't always come when she said she would be coming; letters she said she had written often didn't arrive, and the phone calls were few and far between. Jayne struggled with feelings of resentment and animosity. How could her own mother be so indifferent to her, especially as she was so attentive to the children from her subsequent marriage? But not long after her conversion, Jayne began to understand that it was her responsibility to honor and love her mother, regardless of what kind of mother she had been. She could only do that by forgiving her. So Jayne asked the Lord to win her heart so that she could do just that.

Neither of these is a fabricated story. The individuals are known to me personally. I say this because it is important to show that this is not some lofty, unrealistic, unrealizable theory. As a pastor of some thirty-five years, I can tell many similar stories of how grace has triumphed so gloriously. In such situations, forgiveness is the means by which the Lord undoes all of Satan's doing. Imagine Satan's rage when he realizes that his despicable deeds have not achieved their desired effect. Hearts have not been hardened, lives have not been destroyed, and the Lord receives the glory.

Which takes us back to the South African mother who endured the heartbreak of both her son's and husband's brutal murders. This is her reply about what she wanted from the murderer:

> "What do you want from Mr. van de Broek?" the judge asked.
> [The mother] said she wanted van de Broek to go to the place where they burned her husband's body and gather up the dust

so she could give him a decent burial. His head down, the policeman nodded agreement.

Then she added a further request, "Mr. van de Broek took all my family away from me, and I still have a lot of love to give. Twice a month, I would like for him to come to the ghetto and spend a day with me so I can be a mother to him. And I would like Mr. van de Broek to know that he is forgiven by God, and that I forgive him too. I would like to embrace him so he can know my forgiveness is real."

Spontaneously, some in the courtroom began singing "Amazing Grace" as the elderly woman made her way to the witness stand, but van de Broek did not hear the hymn. He had fainted, overwhelmed.[8]

Do I Still Wish Jesus Hadn't Said That?

Jesus told Peter to "forgive, not seven times, but seventy times seven." Yes, there are times when I wish Jesus hadn't said that. But once again, with tears in my eyes, I am so very glad he did.

---

[8] Excerpted from Philip Yancey, *Rumors of Another World*, copyright ©2003. This excerpt is by permission of Zondervan (www.zondervan.com). All rights reserved. Read the rest of the book when you purchase it from your favorite retailer.

CHAPTER 4

You Cannot Serve Both God and Money

According to Monty Python, "There is nothing quite so wonderful as money." But I think neither is there anything quite so peculiar. So much so that not only is this something I wish Jesus hadn't said, it is also something I don't particularly relish writing about. Money is far more than simply a medium of exchange; it has way more significance than that. In our culture, money gives meaning and importance to our lives. It makes us feel strong and secure. Lack of money makes us feel vulnerable and insignificant. Let's face it: going out with our friends with a full wallet gives us a sense of status. "Because I have money, I am somebody," we think. That's the theory anyway.

The Sunday Times in the UK regularly publishes a "rich list," in which the richest people in the country are identified. The list was first published in 1989, when a £70-million fortune put you at number 92 on a list that back then had only 200 names. In 2010, in order to achieve number 92 on the list which was then 1,000 strong, you had to be worth a staggering £770 million.[9] Wealth, it seems, has gone supernova.

What I find more interesting, however, is how the people on the list have made their money. There are footballers, models, racing-car drivers, online gaming tycoons, pop artists, and porn-industry magnates. It would seem that how we get wealth is irrelevant; having it is what matters more. Having a career that exploits and demeans women and makes sex something sordid leads to more status than having a worthwhile occupation that does not pay out. In our society, wealth is what makes us significant.

The God Mammon

It would seem that money had power in Jesus' day too. The way he spoke about it shows that it was also full of religious significance. And if he could teach on money as he did, despite not living in a capitalist, free-market economy like ours, his words must be universally relevant, and we would be wise to listen to them today:

> No one can serve two masters. Either you will hate the one and love the other, or you will be devoted to the one and despise the other. You cannot serve both God and Money. (Luke 16:13)

The word translated "money" is from the Aramaic word *mammon*. It seems to have carried with it the idea of "confidence" or something in which to trust.[10] The way Jesus contrasts it with God shows that he sees it as an object of worship. The two compete with each other for our affection and service. In fact, so significant is Mammon that there is an absolute incompatibility between it and God when it comes to our service — we simply cannot be devoted to both. Unsurprisingly, Jesus has hit the nail on the head. Or maybe it was my finger, because I definitely winced.

---

[9] *The Sunday Times* Rich List 2010, April 25, 2010.
[10] Gerhard Kittel, Gerhard Friedrich, and Geoffrey William Bromiley, *Theological Dictionary of the New Testament* (TDNT, 10 vols.) (Eerdmans, 1964), Vol. 4, p. 387.

In This We Trust

Money possesses a unique and deceptive power. When we have money, we are able to present ourselves in the way we want to be seen. We can confidently buy drinks for our friends at the pub, go to the hip new restaurant in town, buy the latest Cath Kidston handbag, or upgrade our iPhone — again! We accept advertising's fairy tales: "Yes, that vintage flowered tablecloth will not only make my kitchen beautiful, it will also make me a trendsetter"; "Beckham's latest aftershave won't just make me smell nice, it will make me sexy." And if we are not seduced by image, we are persuaded by security. We want to save money, to invest in a high-yield fund, so that we have what we need in our golden years. How, after all, will we be able to face old age without careful planning and investment?

There is a certain irony in the fact that the USA, the wealthiest country in the world, has the words "In God we trust" engraved on their coinage. In the West, where materialism reigns and the market is king, and where our attitude to money and possessions is deeply religious, honesty should require us to engrave on all our coins: "In this we trust"!

So what does it mean for us to take the words of Jesus on this topic seriously?

Money and Our Heads

Jesus tells an intriguing and disturbing story about a shifty character:

> There was a rich man whose manager was accused of wasting his possessions. So he called him in and asked him, "What is this I hear about you? Give an account of your management, because you cannot be manager any longer."
>
> The manager said to himself, "What shall I do now? My master is taking away my job. I'm not strong enough to dig, and I'm

ashamed to beg—I know what I'll do so that, when I lose my job here, people will welcome me into their houses."

So he called in each one of his master's debtors. He asked the first, "How much do you owe my master?"

"Three thousand liters of olive oil," he replied.

The manager told him, "Take your bill, sit down quickly, and make it fifteen hundred."

Then he asked the second, "And how much do you owe?"

"Thirty tons of wheat," he replied.

He told him, "Take your bill and make it twenty-four."

The master commended the dishonest manager because he had acted shrewdly. For the people of this world are more shrewd in dealing with their own kind than are the people of the light. I tell you, use worldly wealth to gain friends for yourselves, so that when it is gone, you will be welcomed into eternal dwellings.
(Luke 16:1 – 9)

Perhaps to evade the discomfort of this parable, some commentators suggest that, in each of these "deals," the manager was simply taking off his own commission. He wasn't robbing his boss at all, merely depriving himself of what was rightfully his. However, the manager is described as "dishonest" or "unrighteous." Also, the discounts seem too high for that explanation to be plausible. This was a suspicious deal of the nudge-nudge-wink-wink-say-no-more variety. The cunning manager was making sure that people would owe him favors, but using his boss's money to do so.

When his boss finds out about all this, Jesus tells us that he commends the manager. And this is where the discomfort occurs. By saying that the rich man commends the manager, isn't Jesus commending dishonesty? Jesus does not say that the boss gives him his job back. Neither does he tell us whether or not the boss takes legal action against the ex-manager. All Jesus says is that the boss commends the crook because he acted shrewdly. In other words, he admired the man's ingenuity. The boss could appreciate the cunning and devious way in which this conman used his head to secure his future.

Jesus then points out that such people put his followers to shame, because we seem incapable of using our heads when it comes to money. We do not act shrewdly. This dishonest manager used his head to solve the problem of his future; Jesus is telling us that we should do the same.

What's Really Important to You?

Jesus instructs his listeners to "use worldly wealth to gain friends for yourselves, so that when it is gone, you will be welcomed into eternal dwellings." He is saying that we ought to use whatever money or possessions we have for the good of others, and this is how we will secure our eternity.

It all sounds plausible enough … as long as we skim over the implicit heresy! Because it sounds dangerously close to saying that we can buy our way into heaven.

But before we get out the stake or build the fire, let's assume that we do not need to teach Jesus theology. Jesus is simply telling us that how we use our money reveals what is important to us. For most of us, money, and our use of it, will probably reveal that I am important to me. Take this challenge. Make a detailed list of what you spend in a week. Include absolutely everything. Then calculate the percentage you have spent on yourself, as an individual, a couple, or a family. That will reveal like nothing else what actually matters to you. The reality is that most of us spend our money on ourselves and on the here and now. We fritter it away. But Jesus says, use your head and act shrewdly, because how you use your money shows what you really believe.

Financial advisors will tell you that using your head and acting shrewdly means saving, investing wisely, and creating a comfortable retirement fund. But Jesus seems to be saying that we are acting shrewdly when we generously give away what we have for the good of others. Living for the here and now, as if we have no future beyond this life, is a foolish thing to do. The resurrection tells us emphatically that this life is not the end. That is why believers can make radical, self-sacrificial decisions. That is what helps us cope with disappointment, betrayal, suffering, and rejection. We know that we are living for a future glory that far outweighs our "light and momentary troubles" (2 Corinthians 4:17). We do not need frantically to try to secure happiness for ourselves now, because we have absolute happiness to come. We do not need to find our value in things, because not only is Jesus our treasure, but also we have an inheritance that is kept in heaven for us which can "never perish, spoil or fade" (1 Peter 1:4).

So take your money, no matter how much or how little you have, and find creative ways to use it for others.

Use it to:

- make someone a meal or take them out for a coffee
- buy what you need to host a BBQ for the neighborhood
- help a family adopt a needy child
- promote justice, both locally and around the world
- facilitate evangelism
- support missionaries
- help plant churches

The opportunities are vast, limited only by our imagination and gospel confidence. But as you think them through, keep in mind that it is relatively easy to bless those who are like us. How can you give to those who are not like you? How can you show something of Jesus' generosity to those marginalized by the wider culture? This is the kind of giving that Jesus commends, the shrewd thinking that leads to God-glorifying action.

Imagine this scenario: You have just arrived in heaven. As you are walking around, you see a group of people ahead of you talking to an angel. They all turn to you and smile. No surprise in that, you think. This is heaven, after all ... You expect people to be friendly! But then they begin to run toward you, crying, "Thank you, thank you!" over and over again. They are so excited that you cannot get anything else out of them, so the angel eventually explains what is going on. He reminds you that, as part of your church's justice project, a conversation club for refugees was started. You gave money to help fund the running of that club, which was used to buy refreshments and provide hospitality. An asylum seeker was impressed by the welcome and generosity he received, and intrigued by his discussions about Christianity. He eventually ended up back in his own country, but could not forget how those Christians had treated him. The acts of kindness and mercy meant that their words about Jesus had a ring of truth about them. The asylum seeker became a Christian and lived for Jesus and his glory, leading many others to Christ. These are the people embracing you in heaven. They just want to say thank you for using your head, for investing in eternity.

Money and Our Hearts

So far we have been referring to the central character as a "manager." It is not a bad translation, but it may be a little misleading. "Steward" is better. A steward in the culture in which Jesus lived was someone who was entrusted by the owner of the house with the management of his household. The steward paid the bills, gave the children their pocket money, got the plumber in to repair the leaks and made sure things were in good shape. He was responsible for the household as if it was his own. Only it was not his own; it all belonged to his master. This is an interesting, and particularly suitable, illustration for Jesus to choose. To make his point about wealth and our attitude to it, he could have told a story about a wealthy individual. But he chose to focus on a steward. Why?

Because that is who we are, and it is shocking to us. If we are stewards, then nothing that we have belongs to us. So we must stop our thievery of living like things do.

"I can't have those people in my house!" Guess what? It's not your house.

"I can't use my car to run them around all the time." Problem solved. It's not your car.

"I can't use my money to fund that project."

That's right ... It's not your money!

So you and I are stewards in God's household. He may have entrusted you with money, health, a home, a computer, a car, and all so that you will use it for him and his glory. It is as though he is saying, "Okay, here it is; let's see what you do with it. But remember, it is not yours." If I keep my money to myself or use my house as though it is my castle, then I am not a steward but a thief. The God I claim to worship is not conned by my devotions or religious activity.

But why do we live like that?

As we've seen already, our actions expose our hearts. We always put our money where our hearts are. Our money always follows our affections. When our hearts have been seduced by Mammon, we are not worshiping the true God, but a false god, a cruel tyrant, an unforgiving and a miserable master. Mammon promises much but delivers absolutely nothing. Mammon demands everything and gives not even a scent of heaven in return for our investment. Mammon drives us to work all the hours there are, in order to get more. Mammon says, "Trust me with your future; allow me to make you into the person I want you to be." No wonder Jesus pointed out the impossibility of serving both Mammon and God. No wonder this thing is uncomfortable. The god Mammon has won our hearts, and so we serve it with devotion and zeal. The true God just gets in the way of that worship.

Who do you serve? Did you feel uneasy, awkward, or irritated about being told that your money, or your house, or your car isn't yours? Did you say quietly to yourself,

"There's no way I'm going to stop spending 16 dollars a day on cigarettes."

"No way I'm going to stop saving 300 dollars per month for my kids' education."

"No way I'm going to let people invade my home."

"There's no way I'm going to settle for a cheaper, less prestigious phone."

The answers reveal who has your future and what has your heart. But the point of all this is not to stop us enjoying any of life's good things. I am not advocating becoming a self-flagellating hermit. There are wholesome, beautiful things that God has given us the ability to create. Admiring a well-crafted piece of furniture or a unique piece of clothing, enjoying a piece of music, relishing tasty food, being impressed by the engineering and design behind a sleek car or motorbike — all of these things are part and parcel of living well under God's good reign. But when we begin to worship the created thing rather than the Creator, and in our yearning to possess it become possessed by it, we are exchanging the truth about God for a lie.

By contrast, when we use our heads shrewdly, we will use the money and things God has given us to serve others. It is as we put our hope in God that we invest wisely. That is how we store up treasure which gives us access to true life, which begins and ends with knowing our Lord and Savior.

A Changed Heart

John Wesley, the eighteenth-century English preacher, came from a poor background. His father, Samuel, was an Anglican minister who had to support a family of nine children in a poor parish. The family was usually in debt, and as a boy, young John witnessed his father being taken off to a debtors' prison. So when John began earning about £30 a year, which was plenty to live comfortably on at that time, he enjoyed his new-found financial freedom. But then he experienced something that changed his perspective. Charles Edward White tells the story:

> He had just finished paying for some pictures for his room when one of the chambermaids came to his door. It was a cold winter day, and he noticed that she had nothing to protect her except a thin linen gown. He reached into his pocket to give her some money to buy a coat but found he had too little left. Immediately, the thought struck him that the Lord was not pleased with the way he had spent his money. He asked himself, Will thy Master say, "Well done, good and faithful steward?" Thou hast adorned thy walls with the money which might have screened this poor creature from the cold! O justice! O mercy! Are not these pictures the blood of this poor maid? [11]

From then on, Wesley's heart was changed, and his priorities shifted. He set a budget. For the first year, he recorded that, with an income of £30 and expenditure of £28, he had £2 to give away. Throughout the course of his life, he maintained his lifestyle so that he was giving more and more away as his income increased.

Wesley taught three guidelines for dealing with money.

First, gain all you can. Money itself is not evil. If you have the opportunity to make a lot of money, praise God and make it! Secondly, save all you can. Finally, give all you can. Any money left after providing for family and paying creditors, Wesley said, should be given away. We are to be responsible with God's money, supporting the family he has given us and making sure we owe no-one anything. After that, all that remains should be given away for God's work.

---

[11] http://pastorpeterko.wordpress.com/2009/08/20/john-wesley-on-money (accessed July 20, 2012).

This principle undermines our desire to believe that we have done enough if we have tithed our 10%. Tithe or no tithe, everything we own belongs to God.

Thomas Chalmers, a nineteenth-century Scottish preacher, once wrote a sermon entitled: "The Expulsive Power of a New Affection." His thesis was simple and insightful: we can only resist the pull of the world if our love for it has been replaced with a new, more intense affection. Where your treasure is, there your heart will be: love God, and our love of the world will diminish. Love Jesus, and our love of money will evaporate, and our love of adulation, power, and success will fade away. This is a black-and-white situation: God or money? We have to take our pick and make our choice, for our hearts cannot treasure both.

When our hearts are captivated by Jesus and overwhelmed at his abundant generosity toward us, we will give generously. Our solution is not to try harder, but to look to Jesus. In him we see ultimate generosity. Paul puts it so simply and memorably in 2 Corinthians 8:9: "Though he was rich, yet for your sake he became poor, so that you through his poverty might become rich." Jesus expended himself, giving everything, even his life, for poor sinners. Though everything actually belonged to him, Jesus gave it all up on the cross. Let our hearts be captured by this King of outrageous mercy and prodigious grace, so that, through the powerful work of his Spirit, our lives will reflect and therefore commend his generosity.

Do I Still Wish Jesus Hadn't Said That?

"You cannot serve both God and money." I wish Jesus hadn't said that ... but, yes, you've guessed it. I am really glad he did.

Now Stop and Think

We're almost halfway through our look at these ten things which Jesus said that don't sit easily with us. So, before we add another one to the list, let's review them so far:

"Those who would come after me must deny themselves, take up their cross and follow me."

"Love your enemies, do good to those who hate you, bless those who curse you, pray for those who ill-treat you."

"Then Peter came to Jesus and asked, 'Lord, how many times shall I forgive my brother or sister who sins against me? Up to seven times?' Jesus answered, 'I tell you, not seven times, but seventy-seven times.'"

"No one can serve two masters. Either you will hate the one and love the other. Or you will be devoted to the one and despise the other. You cannot serve both God and Money."

Without a doubt, these all fall within the category of "hard sayings of Jesus." But the issue is not that they are hard to understand, rather that they are hard to take seriously! Forgiving someone seventy-seven times? Loving your enemies? Doing good to those who hate you? "Come on, Jesus!" we whine quietly to ourselves (because we know it's not really appropriate to do that audibly to something *Jesus* said), "you've got to be joking!"

A Room with No View

But why do these words strike us as so very ridiculous? We think of them as absurd because they are outside of our plausibility structures. They do not fit inside the realm of what we see as reasonable. Think of it like this. Imagine a room. All you have ever known is life within that room. You have no internet, no television, no radio, no newspapers, no magazines or books. There is nothing to tell you that there is a world beyond this room. Then someone enters your room (a surprise in itself) and tells you that there is a massive ball of fire high above your head, and that all of life depends on it. Should that fire ever go out, everything would die. All you know is an electric light bulb above your head. And, as you have turned it off a few times (after all, what else is there to do in a room all by yourself?), the idea of being dependent upon it for life seems completely ridiculous. So you refuse to believe in the sun. You just cannot make any sense of it. It is utterly ridiculous. There is no room for it in your world, no place for it to "sit" within your plausibility structure. In all of your experience, light comes from light bulbs and heat from a fire that you ignite at the press of a button.

That room is a metaphor for the world we actually inhabit. It is the world of your beliefs and convictions. In your world, when someone hits you, you retaliate; when someone hurts you, you pay back in kind. In your world, far from denying yourself, you indulge yourself. You pursue money (though you'd never admit to *worshiping* it) because it gives you security and makes you "somebody."

That's just the way things are in your world. And mine. Everyone just knows it to be so. Therefore, when Jesus comes and says something contrary, we treat him with the same kind of suspicion Copernicus met when he proposed a heliocentric universe (that is, with the sun at its center). It is not offensive so much as ridiculous. The only reason we might be prepared to consider Jesus' words is because it was Jesus who said them, and then only momentarily, out of respect.

A Brave New World

There are two ways in which we can respond to news or information that threatens to dismantle our plausibility structure. We can immediately reject it (the usual reaction), or we can take time to engage with it and think it through. If we reject it, our existing plausibility structure remains intact. This is the most comfortable option, because life goes on as before. We simply avoid engaging with what has been said and dismiss it as an absurdity. However, if we thoughtfully consider it, we take the risk of ultimate acceptance. This, my friends, is scary. It may end in the demolition of our existing plausibility structure, which is discombobulating, because then we feel vulnerable, insecure, and disorientated.

But then, almost without knowing it, a whole new plausibility structure emerges, shaped and defined by the new information. We inhabit a whole new world where loving your enemy, forgiving offenses, and taking up your cross seem not only plausible, but positively attractive, even desirable. But here's the thing: once we start actually living in that new world, we become an ad for that plausibility structure. Our life promotes it and makes it attractive, or absurd, to others. Theoretically, they think the idea of loving enemies is about as sensible as plunging a corkscrew into your right eyeball. But when they see what it actually looks like, and the kind of community that it creates, they begin to reconsider.

The thing that we need to keep at the forefront of our minds about Jesus is that he is not interested in spicing up my life, or tarting up my existing plausibility structure with a lick of paint and the odd fluorescent tube or two. Jesus is a demolition man before he is a master builder. He bursts into our room and drags us out into a whole new world. He comes to blow apart all our categories and raze to the ground any structure we have erected, so that he can build his own into our lives and make us radically different people. The things we have looked at so far will demolish, redesign, and rebuild our plausibility structure. If we take them seriously, that is.

CHAPTER 5

Keep Awake!

People have all sorts of different techniques for staying awake when they actually want to fall asleep. When I'm driving late at night, I turn the music up very loud and sing at the top of my voice. It's effective both for me and for all the other occupants of the car. I read once of a recommendation to chew ice. Though I haven't tried that one yet, I imagine that the brain freeze it would induce would be a very effective stimulant indeed.

Jesus was insistent about staying awake too, and he encouraged his followers to alertness by the simple fact of his unexpected, unpredicted, unannounced return. Which I think is rather thoughtless and somewhat tiresome. But then it turns out to be another one of those things he said that both demolishes and rebuilds.

"Be on guard! Be alert! You do not know when that time will come" (Mark 13:33). At first reading, Mark 13 seems a little bit obscure and confusing. Mind you, any chapter that includes a phrase like "the abomination that causes desolation" (verse 14) is always going to be a little tricky. The heading in the Bible I use says, "Signs of the close of the age," which sounds like a big deal.

But then, as I read on, I'm left a little confused. There is a strange mixture of what seems to be big picture and small picture. Jesus talks about synagogues and Judea, and says his disciples should pray that it (whatever "it" is) wouldn't happen in winter. But isn't that somewhat geographically specific? By definition, the end of the age will be a global thing, but winter in Worthing is summer in Sydney. Then there is all the talk about a darkened sun, a non-shining moon, and stars falling from heaven (verses 24 – 25). All of which seems like full-on, end-of-age stuff. If the sun is going dark, then it's not only Majorca that's going to miss it.

Twin Peaks

The first thing to get out into the open is that this is not an easy chapter. However we approach it, there will always be questions left hanging. But that's okay. We are not going to make our way methodically through the passage. There are plenty of good Bible commentaries you can look up for that. Instead, we want to try to get to the heart of what Jesus is saying here.

To lay the foundation, imagine two mountain peaks on the horizon. They are different sizes, and sometimes, depending on where you are when you are looking at them, the smaller one gets absorbed into the larger one in the background. At other times, when you have changed position, they can both be seen clearly and distinctly. Both of those peaks are in this chapter. One peak, the smaller one, is a historical event that, for us, has already happened. It is the destruction of Jerusalem at the hands of the Romans in AD 70. The second, larger peak is an event yet to happen: the end of this age and the return of Christ. Sometimes the two events are clearly distinguishable. At other times, they seem to have merged and are indistinguishable. But stay alert, because they are both there!

One of the disciples admires the "massive stones" and "magnificent buildings" of the temple (Mark 13:1). Jesus replies with a shocking statement that every one of those stones will be thrown down. Peter, James, John, and Andrew then ask Jesus *when* the temple will be destroyed and what the sign will be that Jesus' words are about to be fulfilled. So everything that Jesus says in verses 5 – 37 is in response to that dialogue in verses 1 – 2 and concerns the signs that his prediction regarding the temple stones is imminent. Now, if that were the only focus of this chapter, it would be easy. But why does Jesus go and talk about the end of the world, as well as the destruction of Jerusalem?

Because history is, as the saying goes, "of a piece"; it is just one piece of cloth, but with different depths of color. There are certainly ebbs and flows throughout history, but look back over the last 2,000 years and what do you see?

- Wars and rumors of wars (verse 7)
- Nations rising up against nations and kingdoms against kingdoms (verse 8)
- Earthquakes shaking the earth and famines afflicting entire populations (verse 8)
- Christians being persecuted simply for being Christians (verse 9)
- Families deeply divided over the gospel (verse 12)

"This is what it's going to be like," says Jesus, "from now until the end of the world." Suffering is a universal phenomenon, and Jesus' followers will not be exempt from that experience. But AD 70 was particularly acute. Blood literally flowed through the streets of Jerusalem. It was a time of intense crisis, typified by suffering and death, broken promises, shattered dreams, fractured relationships, and disappointed hopes. It seemed so bad that people must have thought that the world was coming to an end. But it wasn't. And it didn't. History had not yet run its God-appointed course. But Jesus is telling us that one day it will, and that we will not need telling twice when *that* day comes. On *that* day, Jesus will return, and he will gather his people in, rescuing them from suffering, saving them from pain and distress, and bringing them home.

In the meantime, his message had two parts: one was for the first disciples, there and then, the other for the rest of us, here and now.

Prepare yourself for the build-up to the destruction of Jerusalem. Watch the signs, keep your eyes open and your hearts soft, and take appropriate action.

But as for the day that ends all days, there are no signs, and there is nothing to keep a look out for, so "Be on guard! Be alert! You do not know when that time will come" (verse 33).

There we have it. That is what Jesus said that I really wish he hadn't said! You can see why, can't you? I would be a lot happier with signs to spot and indicators to watch out for. Because when I see those signs, *then* I could start getting ready.

This may be a bit prosaic, but it seems a little like teachers and school inspections. I know things get pressured when you learn about a visit only the day before, but imagine the ongoing stress if the inspectors could turn up at any time, without any warning. With the present system, at least you have a day feverishly to get everything in order. Similarly with Jesus' return. When the signs appear, I could start taking those events seriously and putting my life in order. *Then* I could really start praying; *then* I would really tell others about Jesus; *then* I would really think seriously about my life and what it is for. But until *then*, I could pretty much do as I please. I could live my life as I want, going where I want, doing what I want, and being whoever I want.

But when you put it like that, it's clear to see that this is not really an option, is it? "Heaven and earth will pass away, but my words will never pass away" (verse 31). Jesus is effectively saying, "Look, I know what I'm talking about. Trust me, I'm the Messiah!" And that is why AD 70 is so important. It happened! Everything has happened just as Jesus said it would. The temple was destroyed, and the Jewish people were decimated and displaced.

History has been exactly like Jesus said it would be, and the experience of his followers was exactly like he said it would be. So when Jesus talks about the end of the world as we know it, then we've really got to listen to him.

Be Prepared

The core element of what Jesus is saying is that those of us who follow him, claim him as our Lord and Savior, are to live all of our lives in the light of his return, all of the time. We are to be those who are looking forward to that time, anticipating it, prepared for it. But how do we do that? Thankfully, Jesus hasn't left us groping in the dark.

"It's like a man going away: he leaves his house and puts his servants in charge, each with their assigned task, and tells the one at the door to keep watch" (verse 34). We have a job to do. As members of his household, we are to keep watch and keep busy doing the things he has given us to do. We can (and often do) launch into full-scale debates about knowing God's will for our lives, figuring out what he wants us to do and wondering where God wants us to go, but actually there is no need for a great deal of debate. We are to:

- love God and love others
- serve Christ by reaching the world
- glorify God by enjoying him now, as we look forward to forever

At one level, that all sounds great. But at another level, I am sure you can see why I wish Jesus hadn't said that thing about staying awake. It contradicts so much of what is true of me and my life.

If I am honest, I want life to be all about me: my fulfillment, pleasure, enjoyment, comfort, and ease. Which all sounds fine and dandy until I realize that option is not open to me anymore. Jesus says our lives are to be all about him. We are his servants, and he is the one with whom we should be preoccupied, and to whom we are answerable. But often we don't get it. We have two principal problems:

1. Stewardship

As we began to see in chapter 4, we don't really understand the concept of stewardship. But it's not just our money that is his, or even our possessions: *we* are his! Everything else is consequential or, to spell it out, everything I own is his because I am his. Paul tells us clearly that we have been bought at a price (1 Corinthians 6:19 – 20). That means that we are no longer our own; I no longer belong to me!

One of the great theological terms of the New Testament is the word "redemption." But in the first-century world in which the New Testament was written, it was an everyday, market-place term rather than a religious one. Its essential meaning was one of release through payment. So a slave would be redeemed, because a price was paid to secure his or her freedom. The Bible shows, and our experience confirms, that we are slaves of sin. Sin holds us in its vice-like grip, and we are helpless. But Christ died to secure our freedom. By his death, he paid the price of our sin and broke its hold over us. So now we are no longer slaves, no longer enthralled, no longer trapped. But this freedom is not ours to do with as we please — a freedom typified by a whimsical obedience. It is a freedom to serve the God who freed us!

That is why everything we own is his, and he calls us to offer it to him freely, in a response of thankful and delighted worship.

2. Perspective

Just as we don't get the issue of stewardship, we also have a wrong perspective. We are so focused on the present, on our day-to-day lives and troubles and desires, that we don't live in the light of the cross and resurrection. We don't live daily expecting our Savior's return. And when those defining events do not figure in our minds and hearts, the present is always going to be about me and mine.

Think for a moment about the tasks you do, the words you say, the things you listen to, the media you watch. Yes, Jesus knows our thoughts and actions all the time, but just imagine Jesus physically walking in on you, right in the middle of an action or a conversation. Imagine the shame if what you are doing or saying is unhelpful and inappropriate. But imagine the delight, in *your* heart, if it is something that pleases and honors him.

Jesus makes a solemn and simple promise: I will be back. Like the Terminator, he means it, but unlike the Terminator, it is not a threat but a breathtaking and reassuring promise. One we can be certain that he will keep. The call, challenge, and encouragement is for us to live daily expecting it, looking for it, and wanting it.

For those of us who are his, that day will not be a day of dread, but a day of glory and gladness! It will be a day when every eye will see Jesus the King, and every tongue confess him as Lord. All those who are truly his will be gathered and brought safely home. Everything our heart has ever desired will be gloriously present, and Jesus will get all the honor.

Keep Awake!

When I was just a small boy, my father was in the Royal Air Force. On one occasion, he was posted to Germany and went away for six months. I was well looked after by my grand-parents, with the rest of my family nearby, but obviously I missed my dad. On the day he was due back, I was determined to be there when he walked through the door. But as the hours crept by, I became increasingly sleepy. My grandfather kept encouraging me to stay awake. Whenever he saw my eyes close and my head droop, he would call out to me to wake up. I don't know what time my dad got home, but I do know that I was awake when he did. It took all my effort (and quite a bit of my grandfather's too), but it was worth it.

Anyone who has driven at night knows that the problem with sleep is that there are times when it seems almost irresistible. No matter how hard you try, and no matter how much you remind yourself of the utter stupidity of falling asleep at the wheel, if you lose concentration even for a second, sleep will pounce, and the next thing could be that you don't wake up! Sin is like that. It creeps up on us, whispers gently in our ear, dims the lights, and plays soft music. It has one intention, and that is our ruin.

So a job comes up that offers pay and prestige, but demands virtually all of your waking hours. It seems so attractive, and the case for it so plausible. But Jesus says, keep awake!

A relationship presents itself. You know he's not a Christian, but he seems so nice. He's happy for you to go to church and might even come with you from time to time. Anyway, you've heard of people who've become Christians in this way. One date won't hurt. Surely? But Jesus says, keep awake.

You know the image is only a click away. One peek won't hurt, and no-one will know. You know you should walk away from your computer. Maybe even ask your friend to pray with you, but you're confident you'll be okay. Anyway, one look wouldn't be the end of the world, would it? But Jesus says, keep awake.

Do I Still Wish Jesus Hadn't Said That?

Be on your guard! Keep awake. That's what Jesus said. Sure, sometimes I wish he hadn't, but deep down where it actually matters, I am really glad he did.

CHAPTER 6

Love Your Neighbor

As a young boy, when I wasn't playing football, I would often be found reading a dictionary. Don't get distracted by the contrast; we didn't have a TV in those days, so the options were limited. That innocent childhood pastime means I have a fond affection for this type (or genre in dictionary-speak) of literature, and particularly so when I read what it has to say about the word "neighbor." A neighbor is "someone living near or next door to a person; a person in relation to others near or next to him or her." I like that. I like it because it sets reasonable boundaries. Reasonable because I think I can mostly manage them. The trouble is, I don't think Jesus consulted my dictionary before he issued this directive. I really wish he had.

The instruction to "love your neighbor" is part of an introduction to a well-known, and much-loved, story told by Jesus. But I'm going to go out on a limb, put my head on the block, and say I think it's incredibly annoying. I'm tempted to go so far as to say that it's ridiculous. People can only like it because they don't understand it, or simply have no intention of obeying it. But it's here in the Bible, and Jesus did say it, so, if we claim to follow him, I guess we do have to listen to what he says. Right?

> *On one occasion an expert in the law stood up to test Jesus. "Teacher," he asked, "what must I do to inherit eternal life?"*
>
> *"What is written in the Law?" he replied. "How do you read it?"*
>
> *He answered, "'Love the Lord your God with all your heart and with all your soul and with all your strength and with all your mind'; and, 'Love your neighbor as yourself.'"*
>
> *"You have answered correctly," Jesus replied. "Do this and you will live."*
>
> *But he wanted to justify himself, so he asked Jesus, "And who is my neighbor?"*
>
> *In reply Jesus said: "A man was going down from Jerusalem to Jericho, when he was attacked by robbers. They stripped him of his clothes, beat him and went away, leaving him half-dead. A priest happened to be going down the same road, and when he saw the man, he passed by on the other side. So too, a Levite, when he came to the place and saw him, passed by on the other side. But a Samaritan, as he travelled, came where the man was; and when he saw him, he took pity on him. He went to him and bandaged his wounds, pouring on oil and wine. Then he put the man on his own donkey, brought him to an inn and took care of him. The next day he took out two denarii and gave them to the innkeeper. 'Look after him,' he said, 'and when I return, I will reimburse you for any extra expense you may have.'*
>
> *"Which of these three do you think was a neighbor to the man who fell into the hands of robbers?"*
>
> *The expert in the law replied, "The one who had mercy on him."*
>
> *Jesus told him, "Go and do likewise." (Luke 10:25 – 37)*

Everybody Needs Good Neighbors

A parable is a story, but not any old story. It isn't, for example, a sweet bedtime story used to tuck first-century Jewish children into bed for the night — not unless they were fed chamomile tea intravenously to calm them down afterward. Because a parable is a story with a sting in its tale. It's a story intended to shock and confront, designed to make you sit up and get agitated. If it doesn't, and you don't, then you haven't understood it properly. Jesus told this story to get under the skin of his audience. It has four principal characters: the man, the priest, the Levite, and the Samaritan.

We don't know a great deal about the man or why he was making this journey. But he is a key character in the story, because the other characters are all judged by how they respond to him. It was a notorious road, and so the listeners would not have been surprised to hear that the man was attacked there.

Nor would they have been surprised by the despicable behavior of the priest or the Levite. Jesus' language tells us that the Levite walked over to take a closer look at the man lying half-dead, before passing by on the other side. The tale of these two religious hypocrites would no doubt have been merely interesting details, greeted by a few heads nodding in agreement or shaking in self-righteous disapproval. Perhaps a bit like you as you read this story? Religious leaders have always been easy targets. Jesus taking a swipe would have been fairly uncontroversial. It's much the same today, is it not? Religious people generally get bad press: "holier-than-thou hypocrites" who become the butt of jokes and the easy target of many a film or soap opera. So nothing too shocking in the story so far.

But there is, of course, one more character to consider. Some versions of the Bible introduce verse 33 with a "but": "But a Samaritan, as he travelled, came where the man was ..." For us, reading the text in English, this sets up a contrast between the Samaritan and the previous two passers-by. We expect that the Samaritan will do something different. In the original, however, the sentence simply begins with "Samaritan." [12] For Jesus' original listeners, the expectation would have been for the Samaritan to do much the same thing as the previous two. After all, Samaritans were scum. They had no redeeming virtues. Some versions of the Bible entitle this parable: "The Good Samaritan," but for Jesus' listeners, that phrase would have put the moron into oxymoron!

Samaritans weren't Gentiles, but neither were they Jews. They were mongrels. So when the Samaritan goes over to the place where the man is lying, the listeners probably thought it was so that he could give him a sly kick in the ribs for good measure. At first, that's where the story seems to be heading. He does exactly what the Levite did: walks across the road to see the naked, beaten man lying in a pool of blood. But then, wham! Just when you least expect it, the sting in the tail: "When he saw him, he took pity on him."

At this point, Jesus' listeners would have been gobsmacked: "You've got to be kidding, Jesus! If we'd known you were a stand-up comedian in your spare time, we might have brought our friends along to listen to you!" Jesus' words would have shattered their preconceptions and prejudices, undermining the values they had always assumed to be true.

The religious no-goods respond to the bleeding, broken man with callous indifference. The no-good Samaritan responds with costly and meaningful compassion. He rescues the man, saving his life at great cost and inconvenience to himself. The two silver coins he leaves with the innkeeper would probably have covered

---

[12] In verse 33, the word often translated "but" (*de* in Greek) is commonly used to connect one clause with another. It is sometimes used to set up a contrast. However, very frequently it simply connects one idea to another, much as we might use "now" or "and." The same word occurs in verse 31 when introducing the priest, and in verse 32 when introducing the Levite. So in the flow of the narrative, translating the Greek word *de* in verse 33 as connecting rather than contrasting is consistent. That reading also seems to fit with Jesus' intent for the parable: it makes the "sting in the tail" (the unexpected kindness of the Samaritan) all the more potent and unexpected.

the man's board and lodging for over three weeks. And he was prepared to give even more if necessary.

You can almost hear the somewhat reluctant and surly tone, as the lawyer cannot even bring himself to use the term "Samaritan" when he replies to Jesus' question: "Who was the neighbor?"

As usual, Jesus is making a radical point. He's saying that mercy, or compassion, is blind. It is non-discriminatory. It does not make judgments about the person in need. It does not set limits on the help it gives. It is not quality controlled or value driven. It is indiscriminate and even naïve. And Jesus is saying that we cannot eliminate *anyone* from the category of "neighbor." He is challenging every preconception that would assume someone is, or is not, likely to be a bona fide neighbor. Like a master swordsman, he cuts through all cultural and personal defenses, so his rapier goes right to the heart of his listeners' self-righteous pride.

Limitless Compassion

Before we can understand just how ridiculous this story is, we need to understand why Jesus told it. Jesus was involved in a dialogue with a young lawyer who wanted to know how he could inherit eternal life. The NIV says that he was trying to test Jesus. But that does not seem to be the case, because, when Jesus answers him with the two great commands about loving God and loving others, the man, "wanting to justify himself," asks, "Who is my neighbor?"

That's a great question, and it shows that this young lawyer had a brilliant career ahead of him. By asking "Who is my neighbor?" he is really asking for Jesus to tell him who *wasn't* his neighbor. This is all very attractive, because it significantly reduces liability. If I know who *isn't* my neighbor, then I don't have to worry about trying to love everyone — which is clearly impossible, isn't it? Everyone knows that, to succeed, we need small goals. If we're going to love our neighbor, we need to know who he or she is. Then we can get the job done and not worry about all the others who would be such a drain on our resources. If I know that I don't need to worry about loving the illegal immigrants, the unemployed, or the homeless, then I can get on with my life without guilt. I can walk past the *Big Issue* seller with no twinges of conscience, never mind compassion. I can look with concealed but simmering disdain at the drunk, barely clothed girls staggering around on the street late at night.

So Jesus tells a shocking story about a compassionate Samaritan, in order to answer a lawyer's question. Jesus is stopping this man's attempted self-justification in its tracks. This man wanted to find out who he must love. Jesus tells this story to show how vast, how startling is the magnitude of the love God expects his followers to show toward others. But if you are still able to read this story without needing blood-pressure medication, let me spell it out clearly:

Even my sworn enemy is the legitimate and necessary object of my compassion.

*Every*one and *any*one is my neighbor.

Compassion and mercy are integral to eternal life.

Nice Theory, But ...

In all honesty, I have to confess that I don't like any one of those three mandates. And when they all come together, I find them completely unreasonable. "What do you think I am, Jesus? A ... Christian!?" There, that's the moment when the sting really stings. That is precisely what I am, and I suspect that the majority of you reading this book are too. We are Christians. Disciples. Followers of Jesus. We are those who want to know about eternal life, who want to be as sure as we can be that we have inherited it. We are those who want to be certain that we are part of the revolution that Jesus brought in. Jesus makes indiscriminate mercy, instinctive compassion, and costly kindness non-negotiables in the eternal-life stakes. It is impossible to follow Jesus and ignore others. If we love Jesus, then we will love our neighbors, all of them, without exception. If we're not loving our neighbors, then we have to question whether we really know Jesus at all.

But of course my problem is that I do not often, and certainly not always, love my neighbor in this way. And I don't entirely understand how literally I should take these words of Jesus.

In the United Kingdom we are blessed with an excellent National Health Service, which provides every single person, regardless of income or background, with the health care they need. So yes, I might call an ambulance if I saw someone hurt along the side of the road, but I wouldn't feel obliged to go with them to the hospital and make sure that they had all the clothes, money, and food that they needed for their recovery. That would just be over the top, wouldn't it? I might drop some coins in the homeless man's tin, or even buy him a sandwich, but ask him home with me to get cleaned up, have a full meal, and maybe even stay for a while? That would be unwise! This homeless person I don't know might harm my family or steal my things. That kind of compassion seems foolish, naïve, reckless. Eager teenagers on youth group mission trips do those kinds of things: well-intentioned but not very thought through. Older and wiser Christians can find many reasons why there are better ways to love these people. And there could very well be better ways to love them. But would that not also be a convenient way to avoid them and keep ourselves safe? The Samaritan was taking a risk in stopping, because muggers could have been lying in wait, ready to pounce on yet another mug! Wisdom is not synonymous with safe; it simply means putting things in place to minimize unnecessary risk.

Indiscriminate Mercy

So what does this kind of costly love for any and every neighbor actually mean — and what does it look like in real life? Here's just one historical example:

In the Netherlands, over four hundred years ago, a Christian called Dirk Willems was being chased by a soldier intent on arresting him. Dirk's crime was that he had chosen to be rebaptized as a willing adult, believing that infant baptism was not a valid expression of personal belief in Jesus. He was one of a group known as the Anabaptists who faced severe persecution — the men were usually burned at the stake, while the women were often drowned. Dirk, knowing that his arrest would lead to his death, managed to escape from prison by making a rope out of bed sheets and climbing down the outside of the building. But he was spotted and pursued. He ran over a frozen lake and managed to make it across, but when the guard attempted to follow him, the ice broke and the guard fell into the freezing water. Dirk could easily have made his escape. But instead, he turned back to rescue the guard who, when joined by his colleagues, promptly arrested him. Willems was subsequently tried and executed. His death via fire is recorded as being long and miserable.[13]

That was mercy. That was costly compassion. That was being a good neighbor.

For us, it is unlikely to be as extreme. Most of us don't face the kind of persecution that makes being a good neighbor so very costly. For all of us, however, being a good neighbor includes how we respond to the hundreds of thousands who are suffering around the world. It will also include our attitude to people who live just around the corner from us, people who are different from us:

---

[13] Thieleman J. van Braght, *The Martyrs' Mirror* (Herald Press, 1938), p. 741.

- Muslims
- Jehovah's Witnesses or Mormons
- refugees/asylum seekers
- blacks
- whites
- Asians
- foreigners
- drug addicts
- prostitutes
- homeless
- disabled
- elderly
- middle class/working class/underclass
- students
- geeks
- liberals
- conservatives

We all have a little place in our minds reserved for a group we call "them." These are the "others." They are usually people we don't know, but we see that they're not like us and we don't like them.

Maybe they sponge off the government in some way, such as having babies on benefits or going to the hospital as illegal immigrants, generally sapping the resources of hard-working citizens. Maybe they're the people from less prosperous countries who take jobs that should go to local young people. Maybe they are those who hold opposite political beliefs, which are dragging the country down. Maybe they are the immoral of society: the druggies, prostitutes, and drunkards. Or maybe they are simply those we don't understand: people with a different skin color and language, different customs, different ways of relating to one another.

Prejudice is a great time saver. It allows us to form opinions without having to consider the facts or gather reliable information.

Prejudice allows us to form opinions without empathy, to make judgments without compassion. This story of the Samaritan, in sharp contrast, gives us an example of truly neighborly behavior.

This incident in Luke's account of the life and work of Jesus is the beginning of a section where he shows Jesus the King, having come from heaven, now on his way back there. He is inviting people to follow him on this journey, which sounds really quite wonderful. At least, that is, until we realize that the return journey is going to be far more arduous than the one that brought Jesus here. The way back to heaven for Jesus was via the cross. The way to heaven for all those would-be followers is also via the cross. Luke is showing Jesus spelling out simply and clearly what it means to follow him.

In this context, the story does two things: one explicit and one implicit. It explicitly challenges us to go and do likewise, because that's the challenge Jesus lays down to the lawyer in verse 37: "Go and show mercy"; "go and be mercy-full." Followers of Jesus are to be merciful, just as he is merciful.

But it also implicitly exposes our sin. Which is precisely why Jesus told it. We all know, don't we, that, for all our aspirations and protestations, mercy is too often not the dominant character trait of our hearts? Too often we default to a works-based response, where people have to earn our compassion. We instinctively create categories of the deserving and the undeserving "poor." We'll reach out to the former, but are happy to let the latter stew in the mess of their own making. But when those attitudes are exposed in my heart, so too is my desperate need of a Savior.

Eternal Life Now

Mercy and compassion are necessary elements of eternal life, because, in Christ, God has shown himself to be merciful and compassionate, so heaven is a world of mercy and compassion.

Eternal life is not just about what happens to us after death; it is also about the kind of life we live before death. In the preface to *The Great Divorce*, C. S. Lewis puts it this way: "I think earth, if chosen instead of Heaven, will turn out to have been, all along, only a region in Hell: and earth, if put second to Heaven, to have been from the beginning a part of Heaven itself." [14]

Eternal life is life as God intended life to be lived: it is life in relationship to him, lived under the kind reign of King Jesus. It not only anticipates, but actually demonstrates, the nature of the world to come. Again in *The Great Divorce*, Lewis writes,

> Not only this valley but all this earthly past will have been Heaven to those who are saved. Not only the twilight in that town, but all their life on Earth too, will then be seen by the damned to have been Hell. That is what some mortals misunderstand. They say of some temporal suffering, "No future bliss can make up for it," not knowing that Heaven, once attained, will work backwards and turn even that agony into a glory. And of some sinful pleasure they say, "Let me but have *this* and I'll take the consequences": little dreaming how damnation will spread back and back into their past and contaminate the pleasure of the sin. Both processes begin even before death. The good man's past begins to change so that his forgiven sins and remembered sorrows take on the quality of Heaven: the bad man's past already conforms to his badness and is filled only with dreariness. And that is why, at the end of all things, when the sun rises here and the twilight turns to blackness down there, the Blessed will say, "We have never lived anywhere except in Heaven," and the Lost, "We were always in Hell." And both will speak truly. [15]

Lewis not only saw things clearly (well, most of the time at least!), he also articulated them beautifully. In this passage, he sees

---

[14] C. S. Lewis, *The Great Divorce* (HarperCollins Edition, 2001), p. ix.
[15] Ibid., p. 69.

the connectedness between this age and the age to come. By calling us to costly and indiscriminate mercy and compassion, Jesus is not setting the bar high or asking us to save ourselves by our works. He is showing us the very nature of reality. This is just how it is in the kingdom of God. We do not claw our way into it by our actions, but our actions now demonstrate that it is the rarefied air we are breathing and the fountain of life we are drinking.

The "Real" Good Samaritan

Let me put it as boldly as I can and ask you a direct question: With whom do you identify in this story? I might like to think of myself as the Good Samaritan, but I suspect that Jesus wanted me to see myself in his portrayal of the religious professionals. My response to the needs of others is often more like theirs than that of the Samaritan. I am so very good at working with a highly selective and frequently changing list of "neighbors" — which conveniently excludes the majority of people. But showing indiscriminate love and compassion to *everyone* in need is my downfall. Frankly, I fail miserably.

This story exposes me. It convicts me. But you know what happens when it does that? I stop identifying with the hard-hearted hypocrites, and see myself as the bloodied, beaten man lying at the roadside. I then turn to the real Good Samaritan — the One who risked everything and paid so much in order to heal me of my brokenness. That is the true power and glory of this story. The God I walked away from comes into my world, with all of its brokenness and pain, and lays it all on the line to rescue me.

If I think *I am* the Samaritan, then I'm going to have no interest in the true Samaritan. I am going to be secure in my own righteousness. I will justify myself and so be in no need of Jesus. And then, just like the religious two, I will walk away from the inn with a smug and self-deluded smile on my face. Who wants to do that?

How much better to be the one that Jesus comes to once more in grace and mercy, to heal and restore in the image of a merciful and compassionate God.

Do I Still Wish Jesus Hadn't Said That?

At first reading, I may wish Jesus hadn't said what he did about eternal life and neighborliness, but when I look at it in the light of the above, I am actually really glad he did.

CHAPTER 7

Blessed Are Those
Who Are Persecuted

In the film *The Bucket List*, Jack Nicholson and Morgan Freeman play two men with terminal cancer who, rather than simply pass out of this world quietly in hospital beds, choose to go and do all the things they want to do before they die.

I suspect that many of us have, in our idle moments, begun to write out such a list: skydiving, moon walking (not the Michael Jackson variety), mountaineering, knitting. But I can almost guarantee that not one of us has ever included persecution in the list, as in "I want to be persecuted before I die!"

In Matthew 5, Jesus makes the surprising and worrying declaration of "Blessed!" over all those who are persecuted for righteousness' sake:

> Blessed are those who are persecuted because of righteousness, for theirs is the kingdom of heaven.
> Blessed are you when people insult you, persecute you and falsely say all kinds of evil against you because of me. Rejoice and be glad, for great is your reward in heaven, for in the same

way they persecuted the prophets who were before you. (Matthew 5:10 – 12)

I am fairly certain that, if asked, none of us would want to miss out on being called blessed by Jesus. But I suspect we are less eager when it comes to the vexed issue of persecution. Admit it. How many of you read the above quote from Jesus with a sinking feeling in your stomach? How can persecution *ever* be a good thing? And how on earth (and maybe even in heaven!) can Jesus say that those who are persecuted are blessed? Especially if we are to believe the Bible version that translates the word "blessed" at the beginning of these Beatitudes as "happy": *"Happy* are those who are persecuted"? Surely you are kidding? I even find it difficult to be happy when I can't download the latest OS for my Mac, or discover that there is no phone signal at the holiday cottage where I'm going to be living for a week.

But we know enough by now to give Jesus the benefit of the doubt, so let's look at this saying and discover why it is actually an altogether good thing.

also Luke 6:22, 23

Persecution as a Mark of Blessing

There are eight so-called Beatitudes in Matthew 5:3 – 12, this being the final one. The idea of blessing is a significant biblical theme. When being blessed, someone would often kneel to have oil poured over their head. It was symbolic of being marked out, set apart, and resourced for whatever lay ahead. That fits well with the idea of being blessed in this section. When we are meek, or when we are those who hunger and thirst after righteousness, that is evidence of being set apart by the Lord. It's not that his favor is on us in response to our meekness, as a reward for our achievement. Our meekness is itself the evidence that the Lord delights in us. It is the result, not the cause, of his blessing.

All that is well and good, until we come to persecution. To

think of persecution as being the result of God's blessing blows to pieces that existing plausibility structure we were talking about earlier. There is no way that we would think of being spat upon, marginalized, ostracized, kicked in the head, or stoned to death as being in themselves the way the Lord marks us out as his special people. At first reading, that does seem to be what Jesus is saying here. Which is at least one good reason to press on to a second or third reading, in the hope that we will find an alternative meaning!

But here's a problem. As Christians living in a multicultural society that prides itself on the virtue of tolerance, persecution does not seem to be all that likely. Perhaps some of you are thinking, "I don't hide the fact that I am a Christian — I walk into a church building every week without attempt at concealment. I even tell people at work that I can't go to the cinema tonight because I am going to a Bible study. Yet all I am met with is an expression that says, 'Whatever works for you, my friend.'" So, if I don't experience persecution, does that mean I cannot consider myself blessed? And what exactly does Jesus mean when he says that the kingdom of heaven belongs to those who are persecuted? As one of the non-persecuted set, does that mean I've missed out on my ticket to glory?

Setting It All in Context

To start unpacking these words of Jesus, we need to understand at least something of the context into which he spoke them.

The first thing is to set these words within the larger framework of Matthew's Gospel. It is clear from the outset of Matthew's account of the life and ministry of Jesus that he is intent on showing how God has kept his promises to his people, and through them, to the world. This is the case in 1:23 where Matthew cites Isaiah 7:14 with reference to the title "Immanuel" or "God with us." This points back to events almost 600 years before, when Israel was exiled into Babylon. This was a devastating event for the Jews. Expulsion from the land meant exclusion from the presence of God. Through Isaiah, the Lord predicted this national catastrophe. But he also promised that there would be a glorious restoration of the presence of God among his people. Matthew shows that this was finally being fulfilled. With the birth of Jesus, the long-promised sign is here: God is once more among his people; the exile is over.

It is no coincidence that Jesus is baptized in the Jordan, the river Israel passed through as they entered the land of promise (Matthew 3). Now Jesus will lead the way for God's covenant people to enter the true Promised Land. The temptation of Jesus in chapter 4 puts him in the wilderness, even as Israel had been tested in the wilderness. But where Israel failed, Jesus does not: he resists the temptation.

So the scene is set for the Sermon on the Mount. Just as Moses (the mediator of the old covenant) climbed Sinai, now Jesus (the Mediator of the new and better covenant) goes up on a mountain. In contrast to Sinai, where the people could not even touch the mountain, Jesus calls his disciples to him. And on hearing of the crowd, he teaches them. This is the new beginning; this is the new community. These are the poor, the mourners, the gentle, those hungering and thirsting after righteousness. These are the ones looking for the kingdom of God, and these will be the ones through whom God will exercise his reign.

From the very beginning, God's purpose has always been to have a people for himself: a people to whom he reveals his glory and through whom he reveals his glory. In Jesus, that purpose is going to be realized in a new and dynamic way, with this small group of followers as the "core team." Jesus takes promises from the Old Testament and applies them to this little band of disciples whom he has gathered into a community under his kind and kingly rule. It is to this embryonic community that he speaks the promise of persecution, and his words are chosen carefully: "for … they persecuted the prophets who were before you."

Can you see what Jesus is doing there? He is creating an inextricable link between his followers and the prophets of the Old Testament. Their role was to call God's people back to covenant faithfulness in times of national apostasy. They were to call back those who persecuted them. Yes, these people claimed to be speaking for God, but so often the rulers and people didn't want to know what God was saying, so they shot the messengers. "This is how it is going to be for you," says Jesus.

Jesus is warning them what to expect as this new community living in the midst of the old community. His own experience was identical to that of the prophets. They tried to silence him too. When that failed, they tried to silence his followers. Not only in Israel, but they pursued them as they went around the Roman Empire.

Time Out

Now let's take some time out here, because you might be catching a glimmer of hope. Is it possible perhaps that the promise of persecution was time-specific? Maybe the ones to whom it applied were those first followers of Jesus, which means that the rest of us can heave a sigh of relief?

Because you may be holding your breath at this point, let me jump in quickly before you pass out. The answer to both those questions is simple, unequivocal, and perhaps a little disappointing: No! It did apply to them, of course, and, as we read the New Testament, we see it being played out. But the principle extends far wider. The gospel calls all people everywhere to submit to God. His people live in the world as a message of hope and judgment. The extent that we are faithful to the King is the extent to which we offer the world an alternative. But in offering that alternative, we are a scathing critique of their lives of rebellion against him. The people of God, through the gospel Word and by our gospel lives, are calling all of God's creation back to the Creator.

In this paradigm of God's people living faithfully under the reign of King Jesus, there is an inevitability about persecution. That is why Jesus points out that the faithful have always been persecuted, and why these followers are to rejoice. It is not some sort of perverse martyr-complex, or a twisted need for suffering. Persecution is the inevitable response of a darkness-loving culture to light.

For a number of years I had the privilege of working with Christian leaders from the Soviet Union, who had been, and continued to be, persecuted by the authorities. Many of them had spent years in prison camps, in cruel conditions, forcibly removed from their families, for no other reason than that they were men and women who loved the Lord and refused to stop telling others about him. Whenever I visited an underground church, I was challenged by their faithfulness, vibrancy, determination, and total lack of self-pity. For them, it was simple: This is how Jesus said it would be, so why should we question him now?

A quick look at history will tell us that this is how it has always been.

A Whistle-Stop Tour

In Hebrews 11, we learn about the cloud of witnesses. Individuals who walked by faith, who, like Moses, "chose to be ill-treated along with the people of God rather than to enjoy the fleeting pleasures of sin." From this "gallery of saints" there appears to be a close relationship between faithfulness to God and conflict with the world. This was certainly the experience of Jesus, the apostles, and the early church.

In Acts 8, we see persecution as being the means in God's hand to spread the gospel beyond the boundaries of Jerusalem and into the world. The church encountered opposition from both Jews and Gentiles. She knew what it was to experience the popular hostility of the crowd, and the official hostility of the state.

Outside the pages of the New Testament, and beginning with Nero in AD 66, the church suffered regular and often intense persecution until the year AD 313, when the Emperor Constantine adopted a policy of religious freedom for all. But even then persecution of Christians was commonplace. For example, in a mere twenty-five-year period between the years 842 and 867, at least 100,000 believers met their death in a wave of officially instigated terror.[16]

Martin Luther, the famous leader of the Reformation that took not only the Roman Catholic Church but the whole of Europe by storm in the sixteenth century, once said, "Suffer, suffer. The Cross, the Cross. That is the Christian way and nothing else." He saw that the history of the church was a history of suffering, and that, while the church lives in the midst of the world, she must suffer at the hands of wicked men.

This understanding was shared by Christians known as Anabaptists, whom we met earlier. The term was a catch-all term of abuse, but many of them were committed to the evangelical faith. In 1527, Felix Manz became their first martyr. It is estimated that, within three years, around 2,000 people had been executed because of their convictions.

One of the pressing issues of their day was trying to distinguish a "true" church from a "false" one. And for these believers, the true church of Christ had a distinctive characteristic, in that it suffered persecution but did not persecute.

In 1553, Mary came to the throne in England. In an effort to reinstate Roman Catholicism, she quickly imprisoned men of

---

[16] E. H. Broadbent, *The Pilgrim Church* (Pickering & Inglis, 1935), p. 52.

conscience, such as Ridley, Latimer, and Cranmer, and began a program of persecution that continued until her death in 1558. Interestingly, when her sister Elizabeth ascended to the throne, although she was a "Protestant," persecution did not cease. It was in her reign that an Act of Uniformity was passed (1559), demanding that all worship be in accordance with the state church, and particularly reinstating the Book of Common Prayer as the only legal means of worship. Consequently, some leaders faced exile and had to endure varying degrees of harassment and suspicion.

I could tell you about the Huguenots of France, the Covenanters of Scotland, the Baptists of the Soviet Union, the believers in Albania, and many, many more. Persecution is not a thing of the distant past. According to one source, more believers died in the twentieth century than in all the previous nineteen centuries combined.[17] And the early years of this century reveal no slowdown.

A famous church leader by the name of Tertullian, who lived around AD 200 and had first-hand experience of opposition, is reported to have said, "The blood of the martyrs is the seed of the church." Although that is a paraphrase of what he actually said, the point he was making to the political leaders of his day was that, no matter how many Christians they killed, the church would keep growing. History has proved him right. When missionaries were expelled from China in 1954, they feared for the cause of the gospel in that vast land, and for the vulnerable Christians there. We know that many Christians lost their livelihoods and even their lives at the hand of Chairman Mao. But we also know that, when China began to open up again, the church had grown exponentially.

As much as I don't want this to be the case, there is something very New Testament about all of this. In Acts 5, the lead-

---

[17] Nina Shea, *In the Lion's Den: A Shocking Account of Persecution and Martyrdom of Christians Today and How We Should Respond* (Broadman & Holman, 1997).

ers of the rapidly growing church in Jerusalem are arrested and brought before the religious leaders and interrogated about their activities. On this occasion, they end up being released fairly quickly, but not before they are "flogged" (verse 40). The word has a range of meanings, but none of them will allow this to be translated as "given a stern talking to." It means something like whipped, flayed, or thrashed. So we should shudder when we read it. But it's their reaction that should really cause us to do a double-take: "The apostles left the Sanhedrin, rejoicing because they had been counted worthy of suffering disgrace for the Name" (verse 41).

The apostle Paul, who himself knew a thing or two about suffering and persecution, wrote these words to his protégé Timothy: "You, however, know all about my ... persecutions, sufferings — what kinds of things happened to me ... the persecutions I endured. Yet the Lord rescued me from all of them. In fact, everyone who wants to live a godly life in Christ Jesus will be persecuted" (2 Timothy 3:10 – 12). The final sentence in the quote is bad enough, but what makes the threatening words worse is the matter-of-fact, Run-DMC tone. "It's like that. That's just the way it is!" Paul was knocking out of the stadium any idea that he was either an exception or exceptional. The word "everyone" is distressingly inclusive and does not easily allow for exemptions. Not even me, alas.

So it seems that Jesus was right. Just as "poverty of spirit" will be a hallmark of a citizen of heaven, so too will persecution. The link between visible faith and persecution is developed in Matthew 10, where Jesus warns the apostles about the difficulty of the road ahead of them. He describes what they can expect from the world. At the heart of his teaching on the hostility of the world is this compelling explanation: The reason why men will hate you is because they hated me.

God's Goodness

So does all this mean that persecution is a good thing? I guess the answer has to be both no and yes, doesn't it? No, because injustice, suffering, and pain are not, in and of themselves, good. In fact, they are unequivocally bad. They will find no place in God's new creation. That's why we should not be looking for persecution, asking to be persecuted, or trying to incite it through just plain, unadorned cussedness.

However, although never inherently good, persecution does not take the Lord by surprise when it happens, nor does it lie outside of his sovereign will. He is a good God who, in his mysterious providence and unfathomable wisdom, employs bad things like hostility, hatred, victimization, and violence for his own good purpose. I appreciate that this may come as a shock to some of you, and you might find news of a pig flying past your window rather more credible. But just think about the cross of Christ for a moment. From a human perspective, that was the direct result of hostility and hatred. Yet Peter tells us in his Pentecost sermon that it wasn't as though the Lord simply responded to the terrible events of that first Good Friday and made sure that it all turned out right on the night. He goes so far as to say that the very act itself, although unmitigated evil, was integral to God's plans to save sinners and glorify his name (Acts 2:23). Persecution is never good, but God uses it for good. He is so wise and powerful that, no matter how bad the ambitions of the perpetrators, his purpose is inversely and proportionally better.

Living Provocatively

I think I am beginning to understand what Jesus was getting at when he said, "Blessed are those who are persecuted." If persecution is itself an outcome of belonging to the gospel community under the kind rule of King Jesus, and if that community is characterized by attitudes such as poverty of spirit, meekness, mercy, and purity of heart, then I cannot run from it, nor even fear it. Those virtues are compelling, and I find my heart drawn irresistibly toward them. Whatever the consequences. That doesn't mean I'm rubbing my hands in glee at the thought of a beating or imprisonment or being ostracized, or worse. It certainly doesn't mean I'm saying with gusto and bravado, "Bring it on!" In all honesty, the thought of persecution still disturbs and unsettles me. But shortly after he spoke those words, Jesus went on to speak a great deal about not being anxious (Matthew 6:25), trusting our heavenly Father for all that we need (6:32), seeking first the kingdom of God (6:33), and not worrying about tomorrow (6:34). Whether I am facing persecution or merely contemplating the prospect, this is a great opportunity to lean into my Father, to experience his care, and rest in his love and mercy.

This is where we now find ourselves. Yes, the persecuted are blessed, but we're encouraged not to be preoccupied with persecution. Instead, we should focus on, and pray for, those other "beautiful attitudes," so that they increasingly characterize who I am as a believer and who we are as churches. In one of his letters to the Christians in Corinth, Paul talks about gospel ministry being a fragrance of life to some people and a fragrance of death to others, both at the same time (2 Corinthians 2:15 – 16). In a world of darkness, the appearance of light will produce one of two reactions. Some people who prefer the dark will try to extinguish the flame. Others who are beginning to find the darkness suffocating will run toward it. As traits such as poverty of spirit and purity of heart are nurtured among us, and as they grow increasingly bright and radiant, we can expect either of those two responses. Probably both at the same time. When that happens, we will know we are blessed because the Lord is at work in and through us, bringing in his kingdom and extending his rule.

Do I Still Wish Jesus Hadn't Said That?

I have to confess that, in the face of this particular thing that Jesus said, I am aware of a stubborn residue of ambivalence in my heart. I don't think I can say with integrity that I am really glad he said that we are blessed when we are persecuted. But I do know that every time I have taken issue with what Jesus has said, he has always been right and I have always been wrong. There is no reason to think that it will be any different on this occasion.

CHAPTER 8

Here Are My Mother and My Brothers

Christians have a reputation for being pro-family, by which is meant pro-nuclear family: dad, mum and two children (preferably one of each gender). Which is why, at the time of release, so many people got hot under the collar when the comedy *Mrs. Doubtfire*, starring Robin Williams, came on our screens. In the closing scene, the would-be nanny responds to a letter from a young girl whose parents are going through a messy divorce. This is what Mrs. Doubtfire says:

> There are all sorts of different families, Katie. Some families have one mommy, some families have one daddy, or two families. Some children live with their uncle or aunt. Some live with their grandparents, and some children live with foster parents. Some live in separate homes and neighborhoods in different areas of the country. They may not see each other for days, weeks, months or even years at a time. But if there's love, dear, those are the ties that bind. And you'll have a family in your heart forever.

This caused quite a stir, primarily because of the way it undermined the traditional family unit. But you could argue that the scriptwriter was simply engaging with the world as it was, rather than the one that exists only in Hollywood happy-ever-after endings. Families, because they are comprised of sinful human beings, are often messy and complicated, infuriating, caring, harmful, nurturing, frustrating, and forgiving — and sometimes unforgiving. They are seldom all that we want them to be, and yet, in ways that we will perhaps never truly understand, they shape us.

For all that is good about the family unit, and for all the commitment Christians make to it, these words of Jesus come as something of a shock. They jar our cultural sensibilities. To be honest, they are embarrassing, particularly when I'm speaking with my more conservative friends. This is one reason why I really wish Jesus hadn't said them. But the main reason for my dislike of these words is that they drastically impact how I view and treat my fellow Christians.

A Dynamic Alternative

At first glance, this statement of Jesus seems to belittle his biological family. Mainly because it does. I realize that many of us will find this uncomfortable, but we simply cannot avoid the force of what he is saying and the clarity with which he says it. Blood ties are discounted and the special status of shared genes is dismissed. In this statement, followers of Jesus are told who their family really is: fellow followers of Jesus. Jesus also highlights the glorious truth that, as his followers, we are welcomed into his family. Jesus calls us his own brothers and sisters. So maybe this is not such a bad thing for Jesus to have said after all?

Let's take a closer look at what he said, as well as the context in which he said it:

And his mother and his brothers came, and standing outside they sent to him and called him. And a crowd was sitting around him, and they said to him, "Your mother and your brothers are outside, seeking you." And he answered them, "Who are my mother and my brothers?" And looking about at those who sat around him, he said, "Here are my mother and my brothers! For whoever does the will of God, he is my brother and sister and mother." (Mark 3:31 – 35 ESV)

In these five verses, Jesus drills down to the deep foundations of his society and plants some dynamite. His words explode, inverting and redefining what family is. The rumbling implications of what he said, like an aftershock as serious as the initial quake, have consequences for every single follower throughout history. Jesus is telling us what family *really* is. Jesus says that our nuclear family is not our primary community. Rather, our primary community is the community of those who follow him. The most significant people in our lives — the people who have the greatest influence and to whom we owe the greatest allegiance — are fellow believers.

In our world, this is shocking. For many non-Christians, this would be regarded as fanaticism, fundamentalism of the worst kind — a social error on a par with the unthinking devotion of suicide bombers or cults that commit mass suicide. Even in the evangelical constituency, it is one of those sayings that most people want to reinterpret. We want to show why it does not mean what it seems to mean. This is principally because most of us evaluate gospel faithfulness based on our fidelity to the nuclear family. A faithful believer is first and foremost committed to their marriage, kids, parents, and siblings.

Of course, the Bible does call us to faithfulness to our families and to our roles within our biological families. Parents are to be honored; children are to be cared for and well-disciplined; wives and husbands are to enjoy a mutual and exclusive intimacy. But a lot of Christians in the West step beyond biblical faithfulness, worshiping the nuclear family instead of honoring it. For so many, the nuclear family is the defining element in our lives. Happiness and purpose are found in our family, and many of us will sacrifice anything and everything for the sake of it. And we do so believing that we are acting virtuously. I suspect that, for many, this is because the nuclear family has become a replacement for church, due in no small measure to the fact that church is often little more than a weekly event or a formal institution.

But Jesus seems to provide little encouragement for that view. His mother and brothers call for him, and he does not even acknowledge that he knows them. He shows no particular deference for his family. Instead, he shows that the claims of his biological family upon him are no stronger than those of the relative strangers with him in the room. That is, if they do the will of God.

A New Family

Earlier in Mark 3, we see Jesus appointing the group often known as "the Twelve," the select band of men he chose to be with him during his earthly ministry and whom he called apostles. Jesus knew precisely the significance of the number twelve, because it pointed back to the Old Testament and to the twelve tribes of Israel. So when Jesus appoints twelve apostles, he is making a statement about reconstituting the people of God under his rule. Just as God originally defined his people and organized them into twelve tribes under the Mosaic covenant, Jesus has the same right to define what and who made up the people of God under the new covenant.

Not only does Jesus, the Messiah, have the authority to redefine what it means to be part of God's family; he also has the power to do so. The miracles recorded in just the first three chapters — casting out demons and healing all sorts of sicknesses — show that this is no ordinary rabbi. So his choice of twelve apostles is no silly posturing on the part of Jesus in front of his followers.

Jesus says that *this* community, which is comprised of those who follow him, is not only the real community that God has been working toward all along, but is also the real family.

It may help us see the significance of this point about church as family if we draw a parallel with marriage. Marriage exists primarily to point to that ultimate relationship. The relationship between Christ and his church is not meant to point us to marriage, as if marriage between a man and woman itself were the more important thing. No, marriage is an intentionally created signpost to demonstrate the all-important relationship between Christ and his church. That order is vital.

So it is with the nuclear, biological family. It was formed as a prototype of the eternal community Jesus is creating. Sibling relationships, in all of their complex mix of joy and irritation, are designed to give us an insight into what being brothers and sisters in Christ is all about. The relationships that will endure into the new creation are those that are "in Christ." No other human relationship exists beyond the grave. Not even that of husband and wife.

My parents got divorced when I was very young. My father remarried a few years later, and I became part of a large, extended family. I was not related to this family by blood. But even before my father was married, the matriarch of that family instructed me in no uncertain terms to call her "Gran." I never had a moment's doubt that I was one of her grandchildren. Even though, biologically speaking, I wasn't. Because of her inclusion, I was treated by the other grandchildren as one of them. All of her other sons and daughters treated me as a nephew. That incredible experience of complete welcome and warmth as a young child has shaped the way I think about family. It disposed me toward an idea of community that is not blood-defined. At least, not by mere human blood! For anyone who has experienced a broken family, the restorative grace of being welcomed into the family of God brings freedom and hope. For those who enjoy a happy experience of family life, it gives a great opportunity to bless others with what you have learned and enjoyed.

Honor Our Parents?

I would be surprised if some alarm bells were not ringing in your head right now. I imagine that you are already thinking of Bible passages that seem to contradict what is being said here. One example would be the sixth commandment in the Old Testament: "Honor your father and your mother, so that you may live long in the land the LORD your God is giving you" (Exodus 20:12). Another example is in the New Testament, where Paul cites that command: "Children, obey your parents in the Lord, for this is right. 'Honor your father and mother' — which is the first commandment with a promise — so that it may go well with you and that you may enjoy long life on the earth" (Ephesians 6:1 – 3).

It is unarguably the case that, throughout the Bible, there is clear direction for children to honor their parents, to respect and revere them, to cherish and care for them in old age. So how does that mesh with these words of Jesus?

Nothing Jesus says here undermines the command for children to honor their parents. Jesus was the perfect law-keeper; he is not going to break one of the Ten Commandments. Central to the Old Testament law was the divine intention to create an alternative and authentic community that would be a light to the nations. One vital aspect of that law was to show that this good society, crafted and ruled by the Lord himself, was where mothers and fathers were honored and revered.

Jesus, by creating a new community, extends that principle. The answer to "Who is my mother?" is *everyone who does God's will.* So, in this new community I'm called to honor, with special affection, those who do the will of Jesus. In this community, no-one is excluded.

A Pulsing, Living Relationship

All those who are "in Christ," the one who is the true Son, are "sons of the living God." We enjoy all the benefits and privileges of sonship. We have been adopted into God's family and are part of God's household. One of the descriptive terms of the Holy Spirit is that he is the "Spirit of adoption." It is his work that enables and prompts us to cry *"Abba."* Isn't that remarkable? But notice the corporate identity. The Spirit does not, in the first instance, confirm that I am a child of God (though I am), but that we are "children of God." We are those who, together, acknowledge the Father, not only as "my" Father, but as "our" Father.

What this means is that the shared identity is definitive of who I am, rather than peripheral. Despite everything society says, we are not the self-ruling individuals we like to imagine. William Ernest Henley got it wrong.[18] The reality is, *we are neither masters of our fate nor captains of our souls.* We belong to one another in a very deep and profound sense. We do not rule ourselves, but submit ourselves to one another under Christ. In Ephesians 2:19 – 21, we have a description of a pulsing, living relationship among believers, through Jesus:

> *Consequently, you are no longer foreigners and strangers, but fellow citizens with God's people and also members of his household, built on the foundation of the apostles and prophets, with Christ Jesus himself as the chief cornerstone. In him the whole building is joined together and rises to become a holy temple in the Lord.*

The language is organic, vibrant, and plural. When one member of this body is wounded, we feel pain too. When one member experiences joy, we rejoice with them. Church is family. We are united to one another in a unique, living relationship, intended to glorify the Father.

---

[18] William Ernest Henley (1849 – 1903), "Invictus."

The problem with all of this is that a lot of our experience of Christianity belies it. Most of us haven't experienced church like that. I'm convinced that one of the reasons why we reject this story as having any particular relevance to us is not simply because we worship the nuclear family, but because of our very deficient experience of what it means to be church. We just cannot imagine it. When church is little more than a meeting I go to or the building I enter, the idea of church as my family is nonsense. When my "church family" are people I see once or twice a week for a total of maybe three hours, it is ridiculous to think that I will submit to, or be involved in any meaningful sense with, these people. Our common inexperience of real, biblical church family is why these words of Jesus sound unwelcome, radical, and disconcerting.

Live It Like Family!

How would you go about making a big decision? Perhaps you pray about it, write out a pros and cons list, talk about it with friends and family, maybe seek the counsel of your pastor. But whom would you count on for good, honest advice? Many of us would most trust and depend on the opinions of our biological family, because they know us so well and they love us more than anyone else does. Seeking the counsel of wise relatives is not a bad thing to do. But don't these words of Jesus show that our church family should speak into our decisions and have a significant influence in our lives?

Imagine letting your personal decisions be influenced by your church. Imagine committing yourself to care for someone indefinitely who isn't even related to you. Imagine opening up your finances to someone other than your accountant. But as shocking as it might seem for us, that is the reality of life in Jesus' family. We are to depend on one another, challenge one another, share life with one another. We are to be willing to have our lives molded and our decisions impacted by our family in Jesus. That is not the same as saying that we do whatever our church family tells us to do. Responsibility ultimately resides with me, as my ultimate accountability is to the Lord. Paul makes that crystal clear in Romans 14:12: "So then, each of us will give an account of ourselves to God." So, if their words contradict the Bible, there is no contest in terms of which we submit to. But if our church friends and leaders are faithfully and lovingly applying God's Word, weighing their words is not submitting to others so much as to our heavenly Father.

I am privileged because all of my now-grown children live within a seven-minutes' walk of my house. God has blessed us with healthy, happy relationships. Two things are interesting to me about my nuclear family: first, the way we interact is influenced and shaped by our gospel convictions. At the same time, what we are as an extended family now shapes my expectations regarding church. For a long time my church has used the saying: "If you do it as family, do it as church; if you don't do it as family, don't do it as church." At every level, that phrase is incredibly simple, so much so that it seems almost simplistic, but it has remained remarkably helpful and instructive.

For example, if you've got a large family, you have to put things in the planner. You have to communicate with several people about what's happening and when. You cannot always be organic and spontaneous. And so in church, we cannot sustain the idealistic view that we are always going to be in and out of one another's homes without forethought or extra food shopping. It is mundane and at times frustrating, but sometimes we simply must plan.

Essentially, I expect that the everyday characteristics of my biological family will be features of the shared life that we're aspiring to, and working toward, in our churches. I am privileged because I have a good experience of nuclear family, but I'm not satisfied with that experience alone. I want that experience to shape and inform how we do life in the new, true family of God. And the good news is that, in Christ, all the blessings of true family are available to anyone and everyone who trusts him. Regardless of your biological family background — healthy or dysfunctional, harmonious or chaotic, nurturing or abusive — if you are a follower of Jesus, then you are part of his family, you belong to his crew, you are one of his clan.

Why It's Worth It

Defining family as those who do what Jesus wants, rather than those in the biological family that I happen, providentially, to be born into, embodies the gospel, because it is only explicable by grace. When I look around the church to which I belong and see the odd assortment of brothers and sisters who are my family in Jesus, I can't help but shake my head and smile. I love and care for them all, but, frankly, many of us would never be friends of our own accord. Only the unifying work of Jesus on the cross, rescuing and redeeming us for his purposes, holds us together. It is a beautiful thing to witness a young student chatting about Jesus with an eighty-year-old woman, or a former prison inmate cracking jokes with a man who has never even broken the speed limit. Only the gospel can bring together people from such completely disparate backgrounds. And only the gospel can cause genuine affection to spring up between those with completely different tastes and preferences.

So do we want to be part of Jesus' big agenda or continue on our own individual, unremarkable path? Do I want to be part of the new community Jesus is creating, which defies explanation apart from grace, and displays his glory to the world, or do I want to default to society's "norm" — that to which everyone else defaults? Real community, formed by Jesus and rooted in him, is alien to our society. Yes, community does exist in our culture outside biological families, but it invariably consists of people whom *we* choose. We join a book group, a sports club, or a Zumba class; we feel an affinity for those who share similar interests and laugh at the same jokes. Apart from Christ, my community consists of people who are like me, and people who like me. And yet Jesus says that true community consists of those who do his will, faithful disciples of Jesus who, according to the "flesh," are a pain in the neck to me. Who just so happen to be the ones that Jesus says are my family!

Just imagine the splendor of our King in the new creation as he rules over his multi-ethnic, multilingual, multicolored people, all singing praises to the One who alone brings unity and reconciliation. Think of the people in your church — those for whom affection comes naturally, alongside those you have to work harder at loving — and imagine each one of them clothed in glory before the throne of the Lamb, fully united in joyous praise to the Savior.

Do I Still Wish Jesus Hadn't Said That?

The supernatural work of grace which binds the family of God together in Christ is something altogether stunning. Anything and everything we hold dear — including our biological families and our ideas about family — can be safely entrusted to this great King. So yes, these words of Jesus wreak havoc with my assumptions and comfort … but am I glad he said them? What do you think?

CHAPTER 9

Don't Be Angry

Marvin Gaye, in a song full of deep pathos, simply entitled "Anger," describes the emotion of anger as making you old, destroying your soul, driving those you love away, and taking you beyond reason. There can be few, if any, of us for whom these words do not resonate. Anger is a universal human emotion. Which is why we should all feel at least a little bit uneasy when we read what Jesus says:

> You have heard that it was said to the people long ago, "You shall not murder, and anyone who murders will be subject to judgment." But I tell you that anyone who is angry with a brother or sister will be subject to judgment. Again, anyone who says to a brother or sister, "Raca," is answerable to the court. And anyone who says, "You fool!" will be in danger of the fire of hell.
>
> Therefore, if you are offering your gift at the altar and there remember that your brother or sister has something against you, leave your gift there in front of the altar. First go and be reconciled to them; then come and offer your gift.
>
> Settle matters quickly with your adversary who is taking you to court. Do it while you are still together on the way, or your

*adversary may hand you over to the judge, and the judge may
hand you over to the officer, and you may be thrown into prison.
Truly I tell you, you will not get out until you have paid the last
penny. (Matthew 5:21 – 26)*

The Ten Commandments are difficult enough. To extend
the command "do not commit murder" to include anger seems
to be a serious case of overreach. God said that whoever murders
will face judgment. But here, Jesus says, "… if you are even angry
with someone, you are subject to judgment!" (Matthew 5:22
NLT). Help! To this point in my life, I am proud to say that I have
managed to comply with the sixth commandment. But the self-
congratulatory pat on the back is stopped in mid-swing by these
words. On more occasions than I care to admit, or even remember,
my inclination to get angry has come all too naturally. I'm guess-
ing that I am not alone here?

Although anger is something we all experience, we may well
express it in different ways. For some of us, it is sudden and explo-
sive. Others of us suppress our rage and allow it to simmer unde-
tected. We also find ourselves provoked to anger for different
reasons. For years, I was unable to watch the film *Mississippi Burning* to the end because I became so enraged by the racial prejudice
and injustice. Yet I am all too aware that I can be almost indifferent to other forms of suffering.

Society advocates different strategies for dealing with anger. A
common piece of advice is that we should vent our anger in a way
that does not hurt others — by taking up kickboxing or squash,
for example. Personally, I find that squash increases my anger
rather than defuses it, but maybe that's just because I'm not as
good at it as I think I am, and so I get frustrated. There are other
proposed strategies to help us find release from anger, such as taking slow, deep breaths and emptying our minds of all those irrita-
tions that make our blood boil. We can always meditate, exercise,

light candles, count to ten (or a hundred if you are really angry), take a walk in the countryside, or listen to calming music.

If all else fails, see a doctor for some sedatives, or self-medicate down at the pub. Yes, we might find that we can temporarily forget our anger in these ways. But all these strategies fail in that they cannot keep us from getting angry in the first place. And, according to Jesus, that's our problem.

Leave the Baby in the Bath

Before we look directly at the issue Jesus addresses, we need to acknowledge that anger is a complex issue. We must be careful not to throw the baby out with the bathwater, because not all anger is bad. When we see injustice and evil, our emotional response of anger is altogether right. We should be angry when tyrants enslave their fellow citizens, or when someone is maligned because of their skin color. A lack of passion here is not a mark of either restraint or godliness; it is apathy of the worst kind: a cruel, callous, and cynical indifference. Getting angry at injustice is a God-like response. Jesus was angry about the coldness of religious leaders (Mark 3:1 – 6), and acted in anger when people were exploiting the poor by buying and selling in the temple (Matthew 21:12 – 13). So anger can, unquestionably, be righteous. I am certain that the anger I feel when I witness racism comes into that category. However, I am equally certain that it all too quickly mutates into *self*-righteous anger. That happens when I regard the actions or attitudes of others as so outrageous that I could never be guilty of them. We are no longer righteously reflecting God's anger at sin, but expressing our own sense of moral superiority.

Jesus is not talking about righteous anger in this passage though. The anger he is dealing with is something altogether different — he is equating it with murder. This saying of Jesus pierces through the outer shell of our behavior. It exposes the importance of our thoughts and emotions, and gets right to the core of who and what we are. Our anger is not trivial. It is neither incidental nor inconsequential. I know this, and it makes sense, but, as an angry person, I still wish Jesus hadn't said it. And as angry people, I am sure that you will agree with me. So why does Jesus say our anger is such a big deal? And perhaps more pressingly, how on earth can we stop being angry?

What's the Fruit?

Anger and fear seem to come from the same type of central nervous system arousal. Our heart rate, arterial tension, and testosterone production increase when we get angry, and there is an increased stimulation of the brain's left hemisphere. It is all part of what is sometimes known as the "fight-or-flight" response and it is hard-wired into human nature.

So imagine living in a hut in the wilderness of Alaska. A grizzly bear decides to call in for a snack, and heads straight for your happily gurgling baby. Here, the fight-or-flight reflex is going to prove very useful. Your instinct is to protect what is dear to you. Adrenaline kicks in, and you are fiercely determined to do whatever it takes to stop this large carnivore from treating your child like the menu of the local take-away. I suspect that few of us have experienced anything quite like that scenario, but it serves as a helpful illustration. The connection between that story and our experience of anger is the instinct to protect whatever is dear to us. What we get angry about reveals what we want to protect and guard. So what we get angry about is a sure-fire way to identify what we really love or desire.

In this passage, Jesus is talking specifically about anger that treats others with contempt. Elsewhere, Jesus says a good tree will produce good fruit, but a rotting tree will only produce fruit that is inedible (Matthew 7:16 – 20). So a good place to start when considering the issue of anger is to look at the "fruit" of our anger. Righteous anger leads to measured, appropriate, and self-controlled action. Wrong anger that sees others as despicable, contemptible, and downright annoying leads to fights, bitterness, and envy. Think about the last time you were angry. What were you angry about? Were you self-controlled or out of control? Were you able to keep hold of your temper or did you lose it?

This Old Heart of Mine

According to Jesus, the heart is more than something we talk about on Valentine's Day. Your heart is the center of who you are. It informs your decisions, sparks your affections, and shapes your personality. And God says that our hearts are messed up. "Sin" is a word that gets a lot of airplay. We can think of sins as things like lying, cheating on a spouse, stealing, and murder, and of course they are. But sin is a far bigger issue. Jesus radically redefines sin by saying that the state of our hearts is even more significant than our actions.

God knows our hearts, and he knows that they are power-hungry. He sees the ways in which we try to hijack his role as sovereign of the universe. We want to call the shots. We kick against his right of control over our whole lives. This same dynamic is evident in so many areas. I remember when I was not-so-sweet sixteen. I was playing in a football game that was being refereed by my friend's father. I knew him quite well and spent a lot of time around his house. He was a good man and welcomed me warmly into his family, treated me well, and fed me often. But none of that made any difference when he blew the whistle and brandished a yellow card at me for what I considered a fair and effective tackle. "You have got to be kidding," I screamed at the top of my voice. I then called him not only an idiot, but a particularly extreme form of idiot (if you catch my drift!). I was so angry, and the fact that he was a competent, experienced, and respected ref made no difference to my utter certainty that I knew better. That football field was my world, and I was god. At least it was until a second yellow card came out, and I was given my marching orders. But that is the utter idiocy of sin. At its core, sin is thinking, "This is my world and I am god." We think we know better than the God who made us, knows us, and loves us more passionately than we can even imagine.

Because of this self-adulation, our hearts refuse to believe God, and instead believe a lie about him. We won't believe that God really is good, and so we think that he will let us down. We won't believe that God really knows best, so we try to grasp for ourselves what we want. James makes this clear in his letter to a group of argumentative Christians: "What is causing the quarrels and fights among you? Don't they come from the evil desires at war within you? You want what you don't have, so you scheme and kill to get it. You are jealous of what others have, but you can't get it, so you fight and wage war to take it away from them" (James 4:1 – 2 NLT).

When a Good Thing Becomes a God Thing

Sometimes we want things that are wrong. But more often, we want the right things too much. A desire to have an affair or steal something is clearly wrong. But even a good desire, like wanting to have an obedient child or do well in our work, becomes evil when we want that thing more than we want the loving God who created us. This is what the Bible calls idolatry. It is wanting, loving, and valuing something or someone more than we value God. An idol can be anything: a possession, a relationship, an ideal, a job. It is anything in which we find our identity or our sense of worth. An idol is anything, other than the true God, that we "need" to make us happy. And idolatry is at the very root of our anger. This is why our anger is such a big deal to Jesus: our anger shows that we are worshiping something or someone other than him.

If you're not sure about this, think again about the last time you were angry. What did you want in that moment of anger? Try to pinpoint the underlying desire of your heart. What do you think you need in order to make you happy? How do you respond when that is threatened? When we are clinging to anything other than Jesus for our happiness, we are acting faithlessly. When we look down on the people around us and treat them with contempt because of how they treat us, we are not acting as followers of King Jesus.

And, put simply and starkly, idolatry does not work. When we worship idols, we find only emptiness, frustration, and sorrow. The Bible says,

> *Those who pay regard to vain idols forsake their hope of steadfast love. (Jonah 2:8 ESV)*

When we try to find happiness by rejecting Jesus and running our own lives our own way, we will find that the idols we crave are false gods, idle idols that will not deliver what they promise.

So, having tried to construct a better understanding of anger, let's go back to the specific thing that Jesus said to see if we are now in a better position to understand why he said it.

It's All About Me. Not!

Murder occurs when the emotions I feel during the initial stages of anger go unchecked due to lack of self-control, or a loss of fear of the consequences. Anger can lead to murder when I dismiss someone and place myself in a superior position to them. I then call someone a fool, a loser, or an idiot. That is what I like to call my "self-justification transporter." I know it might sound a little too Star Trek, but bear with me because I think you will find you have one too! We use it to distance ourselves from those we denigrate as idiots, which then allows us to treat them as someone "other" than we are. In effect, anger dehumanizes them, which then makes the previously unthinkable act of murder now thinkable.

The fundamental problem of anger is that I make everything all about "me." I am the center of the universe. My egocentric heart is wrong, so my attitudes and actions toward others are fundamentally flawed.

But Jesus came to create a new community, where not only is behavior distinct, but hearts are transformed, so that it is now all about the other person. Look at Matthew 5:23: "you remember that your brother or sister has something against you … "! How contrary is that to how matters are usually handled? How many times have I heard, been told, or said myself, "If he has a problem with me, then that's his problem!" I may be prepared to go and sort things out with someone who has upset me (after all, they deserve a piece of my mind), but here I am being told that I need to go and sort it out when I have upset someone else. Yes, even if it was unintentional, if they are being irrational, and even if they took offense for no reason. The initiative to pursue reconciliation is mine; the responsibility is mine. I am forced to think first about the other person. It is not all about me; it is all about them. I am to go and seek them out, even to the point of interrupting my spiritual devotions. I need to go with that resolve and intent: not getting them to see things my way, but to be reconciled.

It does not even stop here, though. It may sound bad enough having to apply this to our "brothers and sisters." However, according to verse 25, we have to apply it to our enemies — yes, even someone with whom we are locked in a legal battle. We are not even simply to deal with the legalities, but to make friends with them. Can you see how radical this is? This is the revolutionary community Jesus is creating to live under his Word.

Liberating Truth

When, in the quiet of our hearts, we despise and belittle someone, it is no different in God's eyes from quietly spiking their drink with arsenic. We are saying that we are better than they are; they have no right to treat us as they have done. Our shaky foundation for happiness and security gets a fatal blow when those around us don't do what we want. We get mad and despise them because they are preventing us from getting what we think we deserve. We so often believe the lie that we are angry because of what someone else has done. But Jesus says that we alone are responsible for our anger. And, even worse, our anger is as bad as murder.

The solution to our mess is to turn and worship the one true God. We look at Jesus' character and see that he is great and good and sovereign, so we don't have to be in control. When we are conscious of grace that rescues "from the pit," we will no longer look down on others, even if they cut us up on the motorway or blatantly ignore the fact that we were standing in front of them in the queue at the Post Office.

The liberating truth for us is that God's overarching control of our lives is altogether good and lovely. Knowing that this innately good God is in control will change the way we respond to situations and people. His character is loving. He cares about every detail of our lives and is intimately involved in them. He is altogether trustworthy. Yes, we see suffering in the world and experience disappointments, but we know that God is good because he chose to take on himself the punishment we deserve for our rebellion against him. He did not leave us to flounder and struggle hopelessly in our sin, but came after us, lowered himself, and died in our place. Jesus, the sacrifice, takes away the sins of his people, and "since he himself has gone through suffering and testing, he is able to help us when we are being tested" (Hebrews 2:18 NLT).

This is the gospel, the good news about how Jesus died on the cross and rose again, defeating death and triumphing over sin.

Following Jesus means that we must face up to our sin, and name our self-righteous, self-obsessed anger for what it is. But what we gain in him is infinitely more precious than the crippled pride we try to protect. Because Jesus, the One who convicts us of the guilt of our angry hearts, also secures the verdict of our acquittal. Our only hope lies in what he has done to reconcile us with God through his death and resurrection. It's his work alone that makes us able to love our brothers and sisters, forgive them, and ask forgiveness of them.

God promises that, in the gospel, he has given all we need for life and godliness. He also tells us that he works all things together for our good and for his glory. He is in control and committed to making us more like Jesus.

When something fails to go according to our plans, the temptation is for us to get angry and frustrated. My wife Janet and I don't often argue. We have disagreements, but relatively few heated arguments. The occasions when we did, when we were both younger, tended to be as a result of the same issue, namely my insistence on inviting people for meals without first consulting her. For me, it was an issue of generosity and welcome. For Janet, it was an issue of managing a tight budget and making a meal for six go around ten people without the resources to buy more food. I thought Janet's insistence on being consulted first was completely unreasonable and controlling. She was stopping me from being a good church leader and cramping my style by interfering in my attempts at being a faithful shepherd of the flock. On one such occasion, I vividly remember being incensed and starting to accuse her of not supporting me and failing me in my ministry. But, as the mist of self-righteous anger was descending, the Holy Spirit brought me to my senses. I saw the stupidity of my perspective, and how I was failing to love my wife well. My plans were being thwarted, and I was the problem, not Janet. That is how we view our heavenly Father. Not as a good God who wants the best for us, but as someone who is out to get us, spoil our lives, and ruin us. We react badly, because his plans interfere with *our* plans, his desires undermine *ours*. But the gospel reveals a God who has a better plan, who alone can satisfy our deepest desires.

We needn't get angry when we don't have what we want — God knows our needs.

We needn't get angry when someone insults us — God's love is of incomparable significance.

We needn't get angry when life doesn't satisfy — in Christ, we have abundant life.

Freedom, Joy, and Beauty

So human anger is an ugly expression of our desire to be in charge. It results in chaos, sarcasm, backbiting, sulking, stress, abuse, high blood pressure, severed relationships. By contrast, the life that God offers through Christ is a good life. Repentance is when we acknowledge that the idol we were worshiping is shriveled and ugly, compared to the rich fullness of joy and beauty to be found in Jesus. Jesus offers peace and joy — indulging in anger only leads to bitterness, pain, and strife. Which will you choose?

Every day, we need to turn away from our self-love and toward the glorious truths of the gospel. We need daily reminders of our freedom in Christ and warnings about the hopelessness of grasping control. God's grace is abundant, and his forgiveness is never-ending. We must look to Jesus and delight in his good control. As his followers, we can trust that God the Father is good, Jesus has finished the work to save us, and that, by his Spirit, he will change our hearts.

These words of Jesus hurt as they strike home. But even as they reveal our stubborn sin, they show us that Jesus has the power to change us. Our hearts can be captured by him and find rest in his control, and joyful peace in his love. As we love Jesus, we will begin to understand a little bit more about what right anger looks like. As we love God more, the things that make God angry will begin to inform our anger too. So the mother becomes angry about abortion or child abuse, in a way that causes her to speak up for the oppressed. The man who used to be most concerned about his status at work begins to care more about injustice in society. As we care more about God's glory than our own, we will care about the things that offend him. Our primary concern, by God's grace in our hearts, becomes that of pleasing our Father. This is a life of freedom, joy, and beauty — this is the good life that brings glory to our Savior.

Do I Still Wish Jesus Hadn't Said That?

So yes, Jesus' words redefining, extending, and intensifying murder do hurt as they hit home and expose me and my angry heart. That's why I wish he had never said them. But in truth, once again, I am really glad he did.

CHAPTER 10

Therefore Go and Make Disciples of All Nations...

In 1967, Frank Sinatra had a hit record with his daughter Nancy. The refrain running throughout the song was: "And then you go and spoil it all by saying something stupid like I love you."

This saying reminds me of that song. At least, the first part of that recurring line.

Jesus has endured the cross and walked out of the grave. Sin and death have been defeated. This is like the best moment in history, ever! Now is the time to party.

This great moment is made even better when we find ourselves on a mountain. We know already from Matthew's narrative that mountains are a little bit special. It was from a mountain that we got the famous Sermon on the Mount (Matthew 5:1). It was on a mountain that Jesus appeared with Moses and Elijah, and God spoke (Matthew 17:1 – 8).

Now we're back on a mountain, so surely this can only be a

good thing. In the wilderness temptations, Satan had taken Jesus to a high mountain and promised him all the kingdoms of the world and their glory, if he would only worship him (Matthew 4:8). But Jesus didn't need Satan. Obviously! Given the location, perhaps the kingdoms are now going to be claimed, and Jesus is now, at last, going to rule. After all, what's stopping him?

You can feel the tension in the air. The sense of expectation is almost palpable. We catch our breath as we hear him say, "All authority in heaven and on earth has been given to me." We know Jesus, we know. Go on!

A Sinatra Moment

But then comes what I like to call "the Sinatra moment." And then you go and spoil it all by saying something stupid like … "go and make disciples of all nations" (Matthew 28:18)!

It seems like Jesus is going to claim the kingdoms of the world. The earthly ministry of Jesus ends where it began in "Galilee of the Gentiles" (4:15f.). From there, the light that three years earlier had dawned so brightly is now to be dispersed into the world. He is God's King and he will rule. But not in an instant. Not with the mere wave of a hand or the simple shout of an order. The kingdom of God, it seems, will be won inconveniently by the disciples of Jesus having to take the trouble of going into the world and making more disciples of Jesus.

How stupid is that? I'm absolutely sure that it doesn't have to be this way. Why can't Jesus just do it himself? The nations are his, so why can't he just claim them?

Here's the thing. Instead of me being able to sit back and bask in the reflected glory of the risen and commended Christ, I am brought into the game and expected to play a part. And not an incidental part either, as it happens. Going into all the world sounds like serious business to me, requiring serious commitment.

But once again, and now for the final time, I know, this is Jesus speaking, and so it is far from stupid. In fact, we know that these words, like all his other words, are life and sanity. Which is why we will do well to pause and consider them in some detail, so that we might know how to live well in a mixed-up, messed-up world.

Although we won't linger here, we need at least to acknowledge that the command to "go and disciple" is lovingly encased in a bold claim: "All authority ... has been given to me" (verse 18) and a reassuring promise: "I am with you always" (verse 20). I mention this because it should at least temper any sense of disappointment I may feel, or any temptation to be overwhelmed by expectations. Okay, so Jesus is not going to do it himself in one spectacular, superhero-like moment, but authority does belong to him, and his presence is a cast-iron guarantee. (We'll come back to this, but do keep it in mind as we unpack what Jesus wants from us, as his people.)

So the command Jesus gave consists of two main elements: go and disciple. The means by which people are discipled are baptism and teaching. In my experience, it's the easy words that can trip us up the hardest, so let's go through them one at a time, just to be sure we don't miss anything.

Go

One word. Two letters. Single syllable.

It is difficult to think of a more accessible word. "Go" is simple, direct, and unambiguous. Go means don't stay here. It means don't hang around. It means don't put your feet up and relax. Not yet anyway. There is a job to be done, and it will only be done if you go. In fact, it is so clear that, if we listen carefully as we sit sipping our cappuccinos, we should be able to hear Jesus asking, "What part of 'go' did you not understand?"

For all of its simplicity, the word "go" gives meaning, clarity, and purpose to our lives. The kingdom of God extending is a big deal. The reverberations of what happened on the cross and what was shouted out from the empty tomb are almost too staggering to comprehend. But the instruction "go" brings us all into play.

One of my early experiences of preaching in the USA was made all the more memorable when Eric Mason, an African-American pastor from Philadelphia, came up to me afterward, introduced himself, and said, "Man, you were smokin' up there!" Now bear in mind that I am a middle-aged white bloke from England. Consequently, I was a little unsure as to whether this was an insult or an encouragement. I must have looked at him with an evident air of bemusement, because he followed it up quickly with a helpful clarification: "That's a good thang!"

It is just possible that many of you are experiencing a similar moment of bemusement. So allow me to clarify in a distinctively English way: this is an altogether good thing! Jesus is telling us that the kingdom of God will come and his will will be done, and we get to be part of it all happening. We are not mere passive beneficiaries. The grace that comes to us in Christ means that we are collaborators in this kingdom expansion. It is not just God at work, but God at work in us and through us.

What the Bible teaches, consistently all the way through, is that God has designs on the whole of planet Earth. That is why the Bible story begins with the story of creation and not the story of Abraham. God's global ambitions are explicit in the command given to Adam and Eve to "fill the earth and subdue it" (Genesis 1:28), as they are too in the promise about blessing the nations, given to Abraham in Genesis 12:3. God placed Israel in the Promised Land to be a light to the nations. Jonah was sent to Nineveh to remind Israel of the Lord's heart for the nations. You probably know the story well, and so you will know that Jonah was a reluctant missionary who needed to go to the depths of the Mediterranean before he would go to Nineveh. But even in Jonah's detour, we are given an insight into the Lord's determined heart for those who were not his people. This theme is sustained all the way through to Revelation 7:9 – 12, where we see an innumerable company of people from "every nation, tribe, people and language," gathered around the throne. The Lord proves that he is no tribal deity, restricted by borders and exclusive attachments.

But how are the nations going to be reached? Jonah gives us a clue: by the people of God going. This command of the risen Jesus didn't come out of the blue and take the disciples by surprise. If they knew their Bibles, they would have been expecting it, because the directive to "go" was written into the contract from the very beginning.

Look at the word attached to the command: "therefore." In that one word, we are reminded of the staggering claim made by the resurrected Jesus: all authority has been given to me. That is why we go and that is why we are able to go. We don't go on our own, under our own steam, and in our own strength. We go, confident that the Lord who speaks has the authority to send us and the power to sustain us. And that is not simply a good thing; it is a truly great thing!

Disciple, Baptize, and Teach

"Disciple" looks like it might be a slightly more difficult word, but it is actually quite simple. According to Matthew 4:19 – 20, a disciple was someone who obeyed the call of Jesus to follow him and gave up everything to do so. Disciples were the ones Jesus was now commanding to go to the nations to make even more disciples. Because they knew what a disciple was, they also knew that the disciples they would make would also be those who would follow Jesus and give up everything for him. A disciple is a disciple is a disciple. You don't get different classes of disciples, such as a "stay-at-home-with-your-feet-up" disciple, or a "prefer-to-be-on-the-tennis-court" disciple, or a "get-back-to-me-when-I've-made-it-to-the-top" disciple. You just get the "follow-Jesus-and-give-up-everything-for-him" disciple. Integral to that identity is the privilege and responsibility of making more disciples. That process will then keep on being repeated, ad infinitum, because disciples make disciples. Simple! But how?

There are two principal elements.

Baptism is an act of initiation, a "way in." It is a dramatic act that tells a story. It speaks about dying to a way of life, a set of values, a constructed identity and a dysfunctional community. It also speaks about rising to a new way of life, a radical set of values, a revolutionary identity and a dynamic community. Baptism at its best is a communal act, not an individual experience. It is how we enter into and experience the communal, corporate, shared life of the Trinity: Father, Son, and Holy Spirit. You become a disciple by becoming part of the people of God.

Here's the thing that we forget too easily and too often. Although we try very hard to do so, it is actually impossible to divorce our relationship with God from our relationship with one another. The two are inseparable, as integral to each other as sun is to heat and fire is to burning. They belong together and need each other. Baptism is about being "born" into the family of God, the context where I am "made" a disciple. It is in the family of God that I am able to care and be cared for, love and be loved, forgive and be forgiven, rebuke and be rebuked, encourage and be encouraged. The bottom line is that discipleship is a family affair, rather than a solitary pursuit. Baptism is the point of entry, the birthing pool if you will, into that family.

Babies aren't just born into families and then left. In functioning families, they are nurtured and prepared for adulthood. For all the talk of peer pressure and the influence of the media, the primary influence on a child, toddler, or teenager is the family unit of which they are part. It is in that context where children are taught and learn values. And how is that teaching done? Most of it is done in life settings, as situations crop up, in conversations as you are out walking the dog or chasing the cat or washing the car. A lot of it is in response to events, where someone has messed up or misbehaved or made an error of judgment. But in all these situations, it's "up close and personal." It's a life-on-life thing. It has to be.

And the primary model is observation: children see how their parents relate or react, and they learn from that. Isn't that the focus of what Jesus says here? "Teaching them to obey everything I have commanded ..." You teach others to obey primarily by obeying yourself. This is not to denigrate or minimize the importance of formal teaching times, but it is to emphasize the need for us to bring teaching off the platform and embed it into life. The Bible is central to our identity as Christians, and the best context for it to be taught is in the setting of life and relationships. God's Word should not just be central to a weekly meeting; it has to be at the heart of all we do and how we relate.

People will learn the truth of justification as they see us living lives that are not frenetically trying to justify ourselves or our existence. They will understand the nature of Christian hope as they see us groaning in response to suffering as we wait for glory. They will understand the sovereignty of God as they see us responding to trials with "pure joy"! The truth of the gospel becomes compelling as we see it transforming lives in the rub of daily, messy relationships.

A Together Thing

Having unpacked each of the key words, I think we are now in a position to draw some conclusions.

Jesus not only intends to claim the nations through disciples making disciples; he wants us to do it together. He sends his disciples out together to make disciples together.

If this is the case, then it is something of a double whammy! Maybe it's because I am an introvert, but I fear this makes a difficult task all the more difficult. Going out on a mission, as some sort of gospel paratrooper, appeals to me. Principally, because it means I won't be hindered by others who do things differently and so cramp my style. But also, because in that solo story, I've got the chance to be the hero. I can be "the man who can," with a business card that reads: Steve Timmis, disciple-maker extraordinaire!

The problem is, I can't get away from the fact that the corporate dimension does seem integral to the task assigned. After all, when Jesus sent out the apostles on what appears to be a trial run or a training exercise, he sent them out "two by two" (Mark 6:7 – 13). The corporate approach to disciple-making also makes sense of the book of Acts. What happened on the Day of Pentecost? We read that 3,000 responded to Peter's sermon, and Luke tells us they were "together" (Acts 2:46). They didn't immediately disperse into the multiple nations identified in 2:9 – 11. They gathered and devoted themselves to the apostles' teaching, which presumably meant that, as disciples, the apostles were teaching these new disciples all that Jesus had commanded. These new disciples stayed together, got to hang out with one another, and were in and out of one another's homes sharing not only food, but also possessions (Acts 2:44 – 46). More and more were added daily to the original 3,000, but they continued to meet in homes and in the temple. As they were doing so, they were learning to be disciples and discipling one another.

What is interesting is that, when many of these Jesus-followers were expelled from Jerusalem in Acts 8 after the martyrdom of Stephen, they went out and planted churches. Being the people of God together was so integral to their experience and convictions that they could not do otherwise. And it was not only the famous apostle Paul who did this either. The anonymous disciples who made it as far north as Antioch did so also (Acts 11:20 – 26).

It's the Church, Stupid!

I think I am beginning to understand the strategy behind the commands of Jesus a little better now. Following his death and resurrection, it was his intention to claim the nations. His death gave him the right and, through the promised Spirit, the might to do so. But it would be achieved as his disciples went out to make more disciples. And that meant new churches, communities of light scattered among the darkness of the nations.

Those communities would be the nurseries for disciples, and the light would shine brighter and brighter as they learned together what it meant to be disciples — obeying all that the Lord had commanded, including the command to make disciples.

But I am wondering if this is why I wish Jesus hadn't said this particular thing. Perhaps my problem is not so much with going and making disciples at all? Perhaps my problem, and maybe yours too, is the issue of church. There is a dynamic about this command. It's full of verbs or doing words: go, disciple, baptize, teach. Each one has the potential to energize and envision. But then it seems as though church is integral to them all, and that's where the energy evaporates. Or at least my interest does! For many of us, church is so formal and static, and has all the agility of an oil tanker in dock. It's where disciples are more likely to fall into a coma than be developed and dispatched.

But even if your experience is negative, don't allow that to be your controlling paradigm. Don't just look at what is and ask why; look at what isn't and ask why not. Commit to being a disciple and to discipling others. Work hard among the people who comprise your church to encourage and "gospel" them.

Here are some ideas:

- Discover some training resources that you can work through together with some of your friends.
- Send your leaders regular updates of needs and opportunities around the world.
- Connect with any missionaries the church is involved with, or contact a mission agency if there is no-one.
- Attend the prayer meetings and pray for countries and people groups that have yet to hear the gospel.
- Consult your leaders regarding a short-term trip, with a view to a possible long-term move.

A friend of mine recently went out to a small and closed country in a faraway region. She has committed herself to the people there for the rest of her working life. She is a gifted surgeon who had a good job, a lovely house, a fine car, and the prospect of career advancement. Her decision to go left a lot of people bemused, and she would often get asked, "Why?" Her reply was simple and challenging: "Why not? These people have never heard of Christ and will not do so unless someone goes, so why not me? My job gives me access that most people don't have, so why not use that for the sake of the gospel?"

Without wanting to detract one tiny bit from the global reach of the gospel, and the call to leave behind everything in order to "go and make disciples," the fact is that not all of us will go and not all of us are required to go. But that's okay, because "going" doesn't necessarily require moving! It can mean *go* into your neighborhood. It can mean *go* to the mums you meet at the school gate, or *go* to your colleagues at work. It can mean *go* to the local rugby club, or *go* to the people you meet at the job center. It can mean from wherever you happen to be, *go*. But it always means *go*. It always means take responsibility, get into the game, love the people you are among, be passionate about the fame of the Savior, and, above all else, *go*.

The Promise of His Presence

Look at the assertion in verse 18: "All authority in heaven and on earth has been given to me. Therefore go ... "! This isn't a suggestion, a memo for our consideration, an idea for us to consider, a thought for us to ponder. You can almost hear the imperative and the urgency. The Commander-in-chief has spoken. What else can we do?

But look at the promise also: "Surely I am with you always, to the very end of the age." What an amazing promise: the intimate, enduring, and abiding presence of the Savior. But it cannot be separated from the command. The Lord's presence is a moving presence, and it is ours as we go. The promise of his presence is inseparable from our obedience to his command. Stay where we are, and his presence is with us no more, for the simple reason that it has moved on!

The cloud and the fire, in the experience of the people of Israel as they journeyed through the wilderness, were visible tokens of God's presence. They kept moving because the Promised Land was their destination. We have to keep going and making more disciples by littering the world with communities of light: men and women whose lives have been transformed by God's grace, through his Spirit in the gospel.

Do I Still Wish Jesus Hadn't Said That?

Do I wish Jesus had never said this? Of course not. It turns out it wasn't a Sinatra moment at all. But then, I never really thought it was. Like every other statement of Jesus we've looked at together, I'm very glad he said what he did. Of course, each one turns my world upside down, but that only means that it is then the right way up. His words are truth and the gateway to life. Every one of them brings meaning and sanity into what would otherwise be a pointless and insane existence.

Jesus is our Savior and King. As his rescued subjects, let us ask the Holy Spirit to dispose our hearts to hang on his every word as we follow him, not only into the world, but also into eternity.